Banking on (Artificial)

Theodora Lau

Banking on (Artificial) Intelligence

Navigating the Realities
of AI in Financial Services

Theodora Lau
Unconventional Ventures
Fairfax, VA, USA

ISBN 978-3-031-81646-8   ISBN 978-3-031-81647-5   (eBook)
https://doi.org/10.1007/978-3-031-81647-5

Cover illustration: Lemberg Vector Studio

This Palgrave Macmillan imprint is published by the registered company Springer Nature Switzerland AG
The registered company address is: Gewerbestrasse 11, 6330 Cham, Switzerland

If disposing of this product, please recycle the paper.

This book is dedicated to everyone who believe in a fairer and more equitable world for all.

To the Dreamers. The Doers. The Humans of AI.

Foreword

The current era of artificial intelligence expansion in financial services marks a pivotal moment in the trustworthiness of global economic systems. As we stand at this crossroads, the book you hold in your hands serves as an indispensable guide to navigating the complex landscape ahead.

The expansion of AI into finance is not merely a technological shift; it represents a fundamental reimagining of how we interact with money, credit, and economic opportunity. From algorithmic trading to personalized financial advice, to fraud detection and credit decisioning, AI is reshaping the financial sector at breakneck speed. This transformation promises immense benefits, but it also harbors significant risks that demand our collective attention, and importantly, our informed action.

As someone who studies the intersection of technology and society, I cannot overstate the importance of widespread AI literacy in this new era. Understanding the capabilities and limitations of AI is no longer a luxury reserved for technologists and data scientists—it is a necessity for everyone touched by the financial system. This book plays a crucial role in democratizing that knowledge, offering clear, accessible insights into the workings of AI in finance.

Theo has masterfully structured this work for us to have a comprehensive understanding of AI in financial services. Beginning with the historical context and current state of AI, the book progresses through practical applications, delving deep into the opportunities and challenges that lie ahead. What sets this work apart is its unflinching examination of the ethical, societal, and environmental implications of AI in finance.

Particularly commendable is the emphasis on responsible AI development. In an age where algorithms can make decisions that profoundly impact our financial lives, issues of bias, transparency, and accountability are not merely academic concerns, but urgent practical matters. Theo rightly highlights, ensuring AI serves the interests of all—not just the privileged few—requires collective action, and that starts with informed citizens.

The exploration of AI's environmental impact is both timely and necessary. As we grapple with the climate crisis, we must confront the resource-intensive nature of AI development and deployment. This book offers valuable perspectives on balancing technological progress with environmental stewardship—a crucial consideration often overlooked in discussions about AI.

Perhaps most importantly, Theo is unafraid to delve into the potential for AI to exacerbate societal inequities and distrust. By thoughtfully examining economic inequality and the future of work, she provides thought provoking guidance for creating a more inclusive and equitable AI-driven financial landscape.

This book is essential reading for anyone impacted by the financial services industry—which, in our interconnected world, is virtually all of us. It equips readers with the knowledge and critical thinking skills necessary to engage thoughtfully in the AI enabled financial services sector. More importantly, it empowers us to take collective action to shape an AI-driven future that is equitable, sustainable, and truly serves the needs of all.

Chicago, IL, USA   Reggie Townsend

Reggie Townsend is the Vice President of the SAS Data Ethics Practice and member of the National Artificial Intelligence Advisory Committee.

Preface

Banking in (artificial) intelligence is the continuation of the Beyond Good journey—one that sits at the intersection of technology and financial services. It is a book of hope, written during times of great uncertainty—a time when hope seems to be elusive. It is also a book about choices—a portrait of our society undergoing transformation led by technological advances and macroeconomic factors.

I am old enough to remember the days when I used to go to the AAA office to get paper maps before taking road trips. I vividly recall the frustration whenever I got lost, desperately trying to navigate my way back. That seemed like distant memories, especially since the proliferation of GPS technology and smartphones. In the past few years, I have become fascinated by the idea of using artificial intelligence as our sidekick. Why can't we treat navigating our personal finance journey the same way, I wonder? Imagine the power of having a co-pilot in our pocket, one that understands not only what we want, but how the changing needs and aspirations of our family and loved ones impact our own financial planning and trajectory. Think of it as a trusted personal advisor who can guide us along the life stages as things change.

The world of data is a world of possibilities. There is power within the bits and bytes that we can harness for good. Surely, we will face challenges. And we are in the midst of another AI hype cycle where many questions loom large. AI as a technology has the potential to greatly change how we learn, how we work, and how we live. Business models will be upended, and new ideas will be formed. Early movers and those with vast resources will stand to reap the benefits. And the divide between the haves and the have-nots will become greater if we are not careful. There are 7164 living languages spoken around the world today. If AI is truly going to be our future, what will happen to the many languages and cultures that will be left behind simply because they are not connected to the larger digital ecosystem and not included in the AI models? Who is not included in this future is just as important as who is included. Progress is not true progress at the expense of the well-being of our society and planet at large.

I am reminded of the dualities of AI that we face. Multiple things can be true at the same time, that AI can greatly benefit humankind, but it can also cause great destruction to the environment and social cohesion. Banking on (artificial) intelligence is about exploring the nuance of the impact and finding balance. It is about facing the constraints head on—from data, to talent, and resources. But most importantly, it is about shining the light on those who are working hard to dismantle the roadblocks—the stories that give us hope. As it is the case with any innovation, we can't progress unless we try. We learn through failures. We fall. We get back up and try again. The road ahead may seem treacherous, but we have simply come too far and worked too hard to give up.

We are just at the very beginning of a transformation and so much is yet unknown. This book is not meant to be prescriptive on the roads we must travel. Rather, it's meant to be the beginning of more conversations across our industry and in our society. I hope this can serve as a bridge to bring us closer together towards one common purpose: To go Beyond Good—to embrace the realities of AI in a data intelligence world and build a fairer and equitable future for all. What happens next lies with our collective actions today.

Fairfax, USA   Theodora Lau

Acknowledgements

Truth is, I never set out to be a writer. In fact, I still do not myself to be one—at least not one of traditional sense. I think of myself as more of a storyteller—someone who explores and narrates. If your eyes are the windows to your souls, then words are reflections of your mind.

I am forever grateful for the team at Palgrave Macmillian, especially Tula Weis, who gave me the opportunity to tell my story. And this could not have happened without Bronwyn Geyer, who has been instrumental in my author journey.

I also want to give a huge shoutout to Reggie Townsend and Brian Lee for all that you do for our communities and for being the beacons of light in the midst of uncertainty. Your foreword and afterword brought me to tears.

Thank you to everyone who have taken the time to share your thoughts with me and guide me on my thinking. It is a privilege and an honor to share your stories.

Thank you to my tribe from around the world, for supporting me through the years and for listening to me without judgement. Especially Penny Crosman, Tiffani Montez, and Katie DeGraff, who have opened doors for me in so many ways.

And most importantly, to my family: I simply could not have done this without you. To the kiddos, thank you for teaching me to dream and to question the status quo. I hope that more adults can see the world through your eyes and learn from you.

To all the changemakers and guardians of AI, thank you.

Contents

List of Figures

1

Introduction

The future will be powered by data intelligence.

It is certainly hard if not impossible to ignore the excitement around artificial intelligence (AI) nowadays.

By the time you are reading this first chapter, this probably feels ancient—which speaks to how quickly the space is evolving. As I type, Apple has just wrapped up the 2024 Apple Worldwide Developers Conference, where they waltzed back into the ecosystem with their response to the generative AI buzz with Apple Intelligence and much-needed makeover for Siri. Just a month prior, OpenAI had their Spring Update with their latest GPT-4o, which is already leaps and bounds beyond the first version of ChatGPT that the team unveiled in late 2022 and sent the world into frenzy. At the same time, Google also announced a radical change to search at their Google I/O 2024 conference that would not only change the advertising model that has propelled the company to where it is today but will also bring about a different future in terms of what we will see and read. More on that in later chapter.

Despite the hype, however, AI is not new. In fact, the concept has been around since mid 1950s. And AI has been employed by incumbent financial institutions and established fintechs for quite a while. In this first chapter, we will explore the history of AI and how it has been applied in our daily lives.

© The Author(s), under exclusive license to Springer Nature Switzerland AG 2025
T. Lau, *Banking on (Artificial) Intelligence*, https://doi.org/10.1007/978-3-031-81647-5_1

What is Artificial Intelligence?

The term, artificial intelligence, was coined by John McCarthy, an American scientist, in 1955.[1] In the simplest terms, artificial intelligence refers to a set of technologies that enables machines to perform complex tasks that previously require humans to do, all the while processing large amounts of data in a fraction of time it would take a human.

The definition of AI was updated by the OECD to reflect recent developments in generative AI. It now reads as follows: "An AI system is a machine-based system that, for explicit or implicit objectives, infers, from the input it receives, how to generate outputs such as predictions, content, recommendations, or decisions that can influence physical or virtual environments. Different AI systems vary in their levels of autonomy and adaptiveness after deployment."[2]

The prominent use of AI is best illustrated by the role that the technology plays in our modern lives. From the moment we wake up when we check our emails or news feed, to when we step out of the house and navigate through traffic, AI is working silently in the background or as a co-pilot in lockstep. As the technology continues to evolve, we'd likely see new applications and techniques.

This is an important moment not only for the banking industry, but for our society at large. Not because we should be worried about AI overtaking humans. But rather, because of the past and present challenges, such as biased data and cost of operations, that could impact the trajectory of where the technology will go, who it benefits, and whether it will bring us together as a society or further divide us.

A Brief History of AI

First, let's travel back in time to 1942.

An American writer named Isaac Asimov published a short story titled "Runaround" in the Astounding Fiction magazine in 1942 and laid out his Three Laws of Robotics[3], which were intended for robots to follow to prevent harm to their human creators. The laws stipulate that a robot may not injure a human nor allow a human to come to harm; that a robot must obey the orders given by humans and protect its own existence, so long as such action does not conflict with the prior law where the well-being of humans comes first.

Soon after, in 1950, British mathematician and computer scientist Alan Turing proposed an imitation game to determine whether machines can think. The game, now known as the Turing Test, involves having a remote human interrogator ask a computer and a human a set of questions, and the interrogator needs to be able to tell them apart based on responses they provide.

Turing went on to predict that in 50 years' time, computers would be able to play this imitation game so well that an average interrogator would not have more than a 70 percent chance of being able to tell machine apart from humans after five minutes of questioning.[4] Though I think it is safe to say that year 2000 came and went, and we have yet to see a machine that can *think* in the way Turing predicted.

The Golden Age of AI

Enthusiasm and hope followed the Turing Test prediction—during a period otherwise known as the golden age of AI. It started in 1956 when John McCarthy first coined the term artificial intelligence during a summer conference in Dartmouth University. Some of the advancements made during this period include:

- Shakey the robot—the first mobile robot to move around autonomously by sensing its surroundings. Developed by SRI (what was then Stanford Research Institute) from 1966 to 1972, Shakey's AI ecosystem was composed of multiple key components, including a TV camera and optical range finder (computer vision), an antenna radio link (communication system), bump detectors (navigational system), and a push bar to move objects.[5] Its layered software architecture was the first time it was used in robotics and the combination with the rest of the technology ecosystem made Shakey the model for future generations of AI-enabled robotic systems.
- SHRDLU—a program for understanding natural language. It was written by Terry Winograd at the MIT Artificial Intelligence Laboratory between 1968 and 1970 and could carry out a simple dialogue with a user to move colored blocks around on the table.[6] Its initial success helped inspire a series of efforts in commercializing AI.

In fact, the field was filled with so much excitement that in 1970, Marvin Minsky, one of the two founders of the MIT Computer Science and Artificial Intelligence Laboratory, predicted the imminent arrival of a machine with general intelligence of an average human in three to eight years.

The First AI Winter

After a series of disappointments resulting from failure in deploying AI in real-world scenarios, however, reality set in. Unlike modern-day AI, access to data was limited, cost of compute was high, and not to mention, there was simply not enough processing power to create or solve anything useful. We will examine some of these factors further in Chapter 4 of the book as cost remains one of the biggest constraints for the adoption and scaling of AI and will impact who has access to the technology and whom it will benefit.

As the saying goes, just because you can, doesn't mean that you should. For technology to be readily adopted, it needs to demonstrate true value and solve a real problem.

A historical moment came about in 1973 when Professor Sir James Lighthill of Cambridge University indicated that "the general-purpose robot is a mirage".[7]

The expectation that we could achieve human-level intelligence in such a short period of time was simply unrealistic. In fact, American philosopher, John Searle, presented the Chinese room argument in his paper, "Minds, Brains, and Programs," in 1980, to demonstrate that artificial intelligence is indeed artificial.[8] Just because a computer program can simulate intelligence by manipulating strings of Chinese characters does not equate to true understanding of the characters themselves as they do not bear any meanings for the machine.

Interests in AI and funding slowed down. The first AI Winter has arrived.

The AI Boom

But the slowdown did not last long. Beginning in 1980s, companies began to adopt expert systems—programs that mimicked the decision-making process of human experts, by leveraging knowledge from experts to answer questions or solve programs, using a series of if–then rules. With potential for commercial value, interests in AI returned, with focus on knowledge engineering.

XCON, also known as R1, was a rule-based system written by John McDermott of Carnegie Mellon University for Digital Equipment Corporation (DEC) to assist in the ordering of DEC's VAX-11/780 systems by ensuring that the proper components were configured in the order. The remarks that John made in his 1980 paper seemed to foretell the future commercial uses of AI: "The configurations that it produces are consistently adequate, and the information that it makes available to the technicians who physically assemble systems is far more detailed than that produced by the humans." (McDermott 1980).[9]

Another notable development came in 1984 when Douglas Lenat founded a project known as CYC, which he dubbed ontological engineering.[10] He argued that the only way for a computer program to have common sense is to import all the facts and knowledge into the program, so that it can process and read, and eventually, understand the meaning of human concepts. "Think of it as the tens of millions of rules of thumb about how the world works that are almost never explicitly communicated. Beyond these implicit rules, though, commonsense systems need to make proper deductions from them and from other, explicit statements" (Lenat 2020).[11]

By mid 1980s, another approach to AI also began to take shape. Started by Australian American scientist Rodney Brooks at the MIT AI Laboratory, nouvelle AI relies on its sensors and the outside world to learn, as opposed to the classical AI, which needs predefined rules and logic.[12]

The Second AI Winter

As the hype increased during the AI boom, the promises of what the technology could achieve did not materialize. The Fifth Generation Computer Project (FGCP), a $400 million 10-year endeavor started in 1982 by the Japanese government to fund expert systems and develop computers with reasoning capabilities, ended in 1992.[13] Unfortunately, the effort did not produce the breakthroughs that researchers had hoped, and it proved to be too ambitious and cost prohibitive. Expert systems required an immense of data to operate and storage was still expensive.

Commercial interest waned and funding decreased once again, marking a brief period of a second AI winter.

The Modern Era of AI

The 1990s and early 2000s saw a wave of technological advances that set the course for the world we live in today. British scientist Tim Bernes-Lee debuted the world's first web page (http://info.cern.ch) in 1991. Marc Andreessen released Mosaic, the first graphical web browser, in 1993. Neil Papworth, a British software architect, sent the first SMS message (short message service) from a computer to his colleague Richard Jarvis in 1992, but it wasn't until 1999 that texts could finally be exchanged on multiple networks.[14] Amazon launched its online bookstore in 1995. Larry Page and Sergey Brin founded Google in 1998 and quickly became the most dominant search engine on the web. Facebook was launched in 2004.

Information exchange as we know it, was changed forever. As the world became more connected, computers became faster and more powerful. The exponential growth of data generated by the internet and connected devices provides the necessary input to train the models. With more progress being made in different areas associated with machine learning, enthusiasm slowly returned.

IBM's Deep Blue, a chess playing computer program, beat the grand master, Garry Kasparov, in 1997, the first time a reigning world chess champion lost to a computer. Roomba the vacuum cleaner was created in 2002. STANLEY, an autonomous vehicle and robot, won the DARPA Grand Challenge in 2005.

Welcome to the modern era of AI.

The Rise of Machine Learning

In 2011, IBM's Watson DeepQA computer competed on the popular TV game show Jeopardy! and made history by defeating two foremost all time-champions, Brad Rutter and Ken Jennings.[15] Watson was a question-answering system named after IBM's first CEO, Thomas J. Watson Sr., and its ability to understand questions posed in natural language and return answers directly represented a big step forward in speech technologies. A new class of conversational assistants flooded the marketplace shortly after, including Siri (2010), Amazon Alexa (2014), Microsoft Cortana (2014), Google Assistant (2016), and Alice (2017).

AI slowly began to take center-stage in our daily lives, anytime, and anywhere.

In 2014, Google acquired DeepMind, a UK-based AI company focused on deep reinforcement learning—a combination of deep learning and reinforcement learning—for £400 million. In 2015, DeepMind's AlphaGo defeated Fan Hui, a reigning three-time European Champion of Go, an ancient Chinese board game. In 2016, the AI system went on to defeat South Korean Lee Sedol, winner of 18 world titles and the best player of that decade, in a match watched by over 200 million people worldwide.[16]

The Age of AI Abundance

Until recently, image annotation, often done manually, was a crucial step in creating the training data for machine learning. Through learning from annotated examples, machines can then make predictions on unknown samples they have not seen previously. Classifying big data can be challenging; the process is extremely time consuming and expensive, and it is difficult to train a model to handle multiple tasks.

There are also ethical concerns as it relates to such data-labeling tasks as well, which often rely on cheap labor from vulnerable marginalized populations. Such exploitative tactics were reported in an MIT Technology Review series called AI Colonialism.[17]

A different approach via self-supervised learning came about around 2017. This new paradigm allows the model to train itself by leveraging one part of the data to predict the other part, eliminating the need for data labeling—a bottleneck from the previous approach. By training with vast amounts of diverse and unlabeled data, AI models can scale more efficiently with improved performance in the real world.

Availability of large quantities of quality data, along with powerful hardware and algorithms, form the three legs of the AI stool. ChatGPT took the world by storm in late 2022. Since then, we have witnessed a wave of new generative AI tools and applications for text, image, and video generation, including Claude (Anthropic), Copilot (Microsoft), Dall-E (OpenAI), Gemini (Google), HeyGen, Imagine (Meta), MidJourney, Sora (OpenAI), Stable Diffusion DreamStudio, and many more. These are only some of the mainstream examples. The ecosystem is evolving so fast that before I wrap up the manuscript for this book, a whole new crop of tools with even more advanced capabilities would have been launched.

Underpinning this new class of generative AI tools are foundation models, including large language models (LLMs) such as GPT-4 and LLaMA that are trained on massive amount of data. Data has often been compared to being the new oil or oxygen. Some also refer compute to the new oil—given how much resources are needed to run the models, a process that is both computationally-intensive and expensive. According to the 2024 Artificial Intelligence Index Report, OpenAI's GPT-4 cost $78 million worth of compute to train, whereas Google's Gemini Ultra cost $191 million.

In this new gold rush, venture capitalists, technologists, entrepreneurs, and big corporations are all trying to capture a piece of the pie, and countries are racing to develop their own dominance in what can be a transformative technology. While the concerns from prior AI winters, including lack of data and computational powers are no longer an issue, there are still plenty of challenges that we must address before we can capitalize on the potential of this new technology. Beyond the staggering price tag to train and re-train the models, environment impact is a big growing concern, and it extends beyond emissions. As AI development and usage accelerate, energy use and water use for cooling will continue to increase, and more data centers will need to be built. For example, according to a study by Shaolei Ren, an associate professor of electrical and computer engineering at UC Riverside, Google's data centers used 20 percent more water in 2022 than in 2021, while Microsoft's water use rose by 34 percent.[18] Separately, the International Energy Agency (IEA) estimated in their report titled "Electricity 2024—Analyst and forecast to 2026" that data centers' total electricity consumption will more than double from 460 terawatt-hours (TWh) in 2022 to 1000 TWh in 2026. This demand is roughly equivalent to the electricity consumption of the entire country of Japan, according to the IEA. While it is difficult to get a precise picture of the exact footprint due to AI usage alone, the projection highlights the urgency to seek more energy efficient solutions. Advances in AI cannot come at the expense of planet Earth—our only home.

We will explore topics including privacy and data rights, ethical and responsible AI, governance, and socio-economic and environment impact in later chapters of the book (Fig. 1.1).

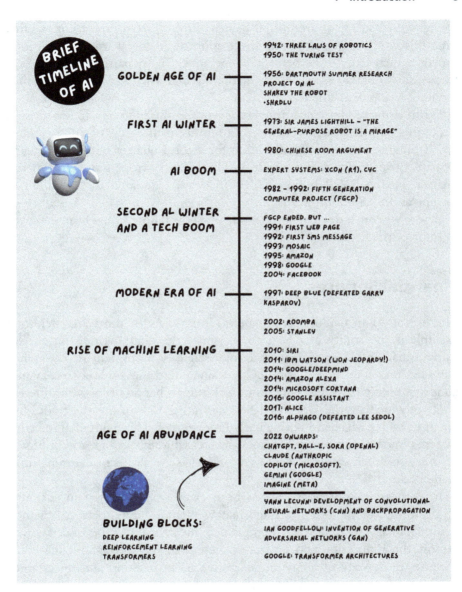

Fig. 1.1 Brief timeline of AI

AI Adoption in Key Sectors

AI adoption has surged dramatically in recent years, triggered by interests in generative AI with the launch of ChatGPT in late 2022. According to "The state of AI in early 2024" report[19] by McKinsey, while AI adoption has remained steady at around 50 percent in the past six years, for the first time this year, organizations that have adopted AI for at least one business function increased to 72 percent. Generative AI, in particularly, has seen tremendous uptake, especially in marketing and sales and products and/or service development functions.

With rising commercial interests, venture funding has followed suit. According to CB Insights, global AI funding in first half of 2024 reached $37.8 billion, including $23.2 billion for second quarter with 948 deals.[20] Perhaps unsurprisingly, funding to US-based AI startups dominates in this quarter, hitting $15.2 billion with 476 deals, compared to $4 billion in Europe and $2.8 billion in Asia.

Before we conclude this first chapter, let's look at how AI has been deployed in some of the key sectors.

Financial Services

The use of AI in banking is not new. Going back in time, an interesting example is the ability of ATMs to recognize the digits written on checks, using a machine learning technique pioneered by prominent AI researcher, Yuan LeCun. In the late 1980s, LeCun trained machines on how to recognize handwritten digits using examples of real human handwriting with different styles provided by the US Postal Service, rather than using the traditional attempts to describe handwriting with discrete rules. This method of inferring patterns in data represented a significant breakthrough and greatly improved accuracy so much so it was deployed for ATMs everywhere to automatically read checks.[21]

In the past two decades, AI has been extensively deployed in customer acquisition, customer service, fraud management, lending, personal finance, wealth management, risk and compliance, insurance, and beyond. We will explore the application and impact of these use cases throughout the book. Despite the novelty of applying generative AI in banking and uncertainty, there is a sense of cautious optimism when it comes to the technology's potential impact on the future of our industry.

Beyond financial services, there are many other use cases of AI in various sectors that are worth exploring, from healthcare and agriculture to autonomous driving, retail, and beyond. Since the list is too long and grows by the day, I will share a few of them in the section that follows.

Healthcare

Beyond financial services, healthcare is one of the key areas where AI shows tremendous potential, with use cases including drug discovery, disease diagnosis, health monitoring, and precision medicine. Beyond automating time-consuming tasks, a common use case today, AI could bring in new capabilities in improving patient experience and transforming medicine.

Take drug discovery as an example. Finding and experimenting with new drugs requires extensive investment in money and time, and the process often has a high failure rate. By contrast, AI can be used to run billions of simulations and analyze massive amount of data to generate useful insights, resulting in potentially shorter drug development time with a lower cost and a higher success rate.

A great example was the COVID-10 pandemic, where AI has played an instrumental role in addressing some of the challenges posed by the virus. One of the more visual artifacts include the use of drones to deliver food, self-driving robots to disinfect hospital rooms, offices, and shopping malls with UV rays, and social robots to communicate and interact with patients, children, and older adults. Behind the scenes, scientists at Pfizer were able to leverage a new machine learning tool to speed up the review of clinical trial data, and hence, the development of vaccine.[22]

Perhaps as a sign of the new future to come, the chemistry Nobel Prize in 2024 was awarded to US biochemist David Baker, and Google Deep-Mind scientists Sir Demis Hassabis and John Jumper, recognizing their work on developing AlphaFold, an AI system that predicts the 3D structure of proteins. This can help to accelerate drug discovery and find cures for other medical challenges.[23]

Separately, connected care is another area where AI has great potential in the long run. Imagine the data from the ecosystem of devices including wearables and sensors being fed to a unified data platform, where all our structured and unstructured data (e.g. electronic health records) reside. Can we envision a future where AI can help us maintain a healthy lifestyle and alert us of any anomalies that will require intervention? Taking it one step further, what if AI can work with our healthcare provider and create a personalized plan to get us back on track?

In a world where the line between digital and human becomes increasingly blurry, how do we best determine what can be *replaced* by technology versus what should remain human, especially for practices as sensitive as mental health for example? Can an AI therapist provide reliable and effective mental health advice? What about the human relationship between the client and the therapist that is typically regarded as essential to mental health treatment? How will that transform in the age of digital?

As with the financial services industry, healthcare is a regulated industry. As such, beyond common challenges around AI deployment, such as access to quality data, care must be taken around patient safety and regulatory requirements.

Agriculture

With increased challenges stemming from climate crisis and growing population, will technology be the answer to improving environmental resilience in farming and achieving better outcomes?

Modern-day connectivity has enabled more cutting-edge technologies to be adopted to optimize productivity and yields. In the US for example, the US Department of Agriculture (USDA) is partnering with University of Illinois to conduct research on how low-cost intelligent robots, coupled with sensor networks and edge-cloud connectivity to help harvest, weed, and manage crops, to alleviate labor shortage and promote autonomous farming.

Elsewhere in India, Outgrow, part of Waycool Foods and Products, provides an AI-based platform that helps their network of more than 200,000 farmers predict and detect crop disease in real-time, test soil health, and know how and when to irrigate, to improve yield with optimal resource while minimizing losses. Promoting resilient agricultural practices is crucial in a world where over 783 million people are facing chronic hunger due to conflicts, climate crisis, and rising fertilizer prices.[24]

Satellite remote sensing technologies can also be used to identify the crop types and yield, which enables digital banks such as MYbank to assess potential credit risks more accurately when extending collateral-free loans to small hold farmers. We will explore the topic of AI and financial inclusion in more detail in the next chapter.

Autonomous Driving

If you are in a major US city such as San Francisco, autonomous vehicles are perhaps one of the more prominent daily use cases of AI.

At the time of writing, however, three major self-driving car companies, including Waymo (operated by Alphabet), Zoox (operated by Amazon), and Cruise (owned by General Motors) are facing federal investigations by the

National Highway Traffic Safety Administration (NHTSA) due to crashes and safety concerns. In one incident in Phoenix, a self-driving Waymo, without a driver present, ran a red light and drove into a lane of oncoming traffic.[25]

This brings up the question that is worth pondering: How much risks are we willing to accept? Are we looking for autonomous vehicles to operate with absolutely zero defect? Or would we be willing to accept an AI system that operates close to human driving? How safe is *safe*? Who will set the guardrails and who will be able to hold the operators accountable in the absence of updated federal regulations? We will explore the topic of ethics and responsible AI in later sections of the book.

But while the progress may feel slower at times for autonomous vehicles for consumers, the potential is vast for automated logistics.

Supply Chain

Japan, for instance, is looking to construct a 310-mile-long underground loop between Tokyo and Osaka. With an estimated cost of 3.7 trillion JPY, it is envisioned that the tunnel could transport e-commerce packages, daily necessities, as well as agriculture products between the two cities using fully automated, electric-powered pallets that can carry up to a ton of cargo each.[26] Aside from potential environmental benefits, this could also help alleviate the growing labor shortage faced in the aging nation.

Similar logistics and micro-distribution projects under consideration include the Cargo sous terrain network in Switzerland that will act as an automatic conveyor system, using automated, driverless transport vehicles to pick up and deliver goods at designated hubs.[27] Although costs remain a concern, such concepts will likely gain more traction as we continue to look for ways to reduce greenhouse emissions and congestion on the road.

AI is also increasingly being deployed to improve supply chain efficiencies. Penske's fleet benchmarking tool, Catalyst AI, for example, enables companies to compare their fleets against other similar ones, and gain data-driven insights into fleet utilization and efficiencies to identify new opportunities for improvement.

Against the backdrop of extended economic uncertainty, working capital optimization is another crucial area for companies as they balance the need to maintain financial resilience and liquidity while investing for future and strategic growth. Advanced forecasting tools can help companies identify cost-saving opportunities to lower operating costs. Cashflow prediction tools can help businesses predict when a customer is most likely to pay, along with their risk of non-payment. Together with automated collections and dispute management, businesses can plan proactively and minimize revenue disruptions.

Retail and Entertainment

One of the most well-known use cases of AI-based recommendation engines lies with retail and entertainment industries. Retail product recommenders based on past purchase behavior (e.g. Amazon) and content platform recommendation engines based on clicks and engagement behaviors (e.g. YouTube and TikTok) are all examples of AI at work in the background, learning our behaviors to provide more personalized and sticky customer experience.

According to the report titled "2024 Consumer Study: Revolutionize retail with AI everywhere" by IBM, most consumers are interested in using AI to research products, look for promotions and reviews, and get answers or issues resolved.[28] Take retailer Uniqlo's shopping experience for example. Using the virtual shopping assistant, IQ, shoppers can receive personalized recommendations, find the right fit, and get support after the purchase. In fact, conversational chatbots are increasingly table stakes for retailers, helping them stay more engaged by extending the touchpoints with shoppers across the customer journey.

AI can also be used to create new shopping experience with customers. IKEA, for example, offers their customers the ability to design their rooms virtually by creating interactive 3D replicas of their rooms and outfitting them with IKEA furniture. Imagine the ability to visualize and share design ideas with friends and family—at your fingertips, anywhere and anytime.

It should be noted, however, that these external-facing applications do carry challenges that still need to be resolved. And missteps can have financial consequences. In a case where the Air Canada chatbot provided inaccurate bereavement fare information to a customer, the airline argued that they should not be held liable for damages as the bot should be responsible for its own actions. Ultimately, the Civil Resolution Tribunal ruled in favor of the passenger and ordered the airline to compensate the passenger for negligent misrepresentation.[29]

Such AI hallucinations are not uncommon unfortunately, since most large language models simply predict the next word in a sequence to make up a sentence. In other words, instead of relying on *truth* (since it does not understand right or wrong), it chooses each word based on statistics. As you can imagine, the consequence of AI making a wrong movie recommendation is different than when it makes a wrong financial recommendation. But whose fault is it when AI hallucinates? Should it be the responsibility of the company that creates and trains the model, or is it the job of the service provider who implements it? More importantly, can it even be fixed? It would appear the jury is still out as Vienna-based nonprofit noyb filed a data protection complaint against OpenAI with the Austrian DPA, accusing the company of violating GDPR, due to its inability to reliably produce accurate and transparent information about individuals.[30]

Regardless of setbacks and challenges, one thing remains certain: The AI train is going full steam ahead.

We will dive deeper on the topics of transparency, trust, and responsibility later in the book, as trust is the cornerstone of the financial services industry and our society.

The iPhone Moment

While artificial intelligence has stolen the headlines for the past two years, and what we have witnessed is simply extraordinary, I believe the true potential lies not just in the impact of the technology itself, but more so what the technology can enable.

Think back for a moment when the iPhone was launched. The new form factor and the new way of accessing information was exciting but costly. I remember my cell phone bill with the hefty data roaming charges after I returned from a work trip right. It was a novelty, but back then, I couldn't have envisioned the new business models and companies that it had enabled, many of which we take for granted today. And it was dismissed by many in the tech industries, including Apple's rivals, Microsoft, Nokia, and RIM.

From banking, mobile commerce, and healthcare, to entertainment, transportation and beyond, none of the new ways of working and living could have happened, and at the pace that it did, without the iPhone and the underlying network connectivity and the vast ecosystem of applications. Rising popularity of mobile devices and affordability of mobile internet, along with advancement in technology and an evolving global commerce and banking system, has not only changed how we bank and consume services, but also enabled development of new business models and new platform players. Will AI play that same role in empowering new innovations? Can the technology be the iPhone moment of our time?

As Mark Weiser once said, "The most profound technologies are those that disappear. They weave themselves into the fabric of everyday life until they are indistinguishable from it."[31] Will AI become embedded into our daily routines and work quietly in the background until it is barely noticeable anymore?

As we continue to navigate the ocean of data, the tools at our disposal have enabled us to gain valuable insights to guide our decision-making and power innovation. But we are merely touching the surface of what this powerful technology can do. As AI continues to evolve along with new use cases, what role it will play in our collective future and who it will serve matters. Who will have a voice in shaping how it is used and how will it impact our society and generations to come? And what will become of humanity when every aspect of our lives becomes optimized by algorithms?

What is our shared responsibility to our society, our planet, and our future generations?

Spotlight on NVIDIA
Based on conversation with Kevin Levitt, Global Director, Financial Services at NVIDIA

Is artificial intelligence the new oil? Is it the most disruptive innovation since fire?

In one of the NVIDIA trailers, the company describes AI as a translator, a healer, a visionary, a helper, a transformer, a trainer, and a navigator. Kevin Levitt, Global Director, Financial Services at NVIDIA, puts it more succinctly: It is the dawn of a new industrial revolution.

There is no doubt that AI will promote unprecedented growth across industries worldwide. From finance, healthcare, retail, and telecommunications, to media & entertainment, manufacturing, energy, and public sector, the opportunities are endless. The speed at which NVIDIA's partner ecosystem is expanding serves as a testament to how far-reaching the impact of the technology can be.

Ultimately, it is not about what AI is, or isn't; rather, it is what it can enable: Business process automation, productivity gains, and exponential innovation in ways we could not have imagined. Indeed, according to Kevin, one of the most exciting aspects of AI in financial services is that there isn't a silver bullet use case; there are hundreds of use cases today that banks are operating against and there will be thousands in the future. And it is clear that banks are already investing in building AI factories to enable their most expensive resources, including data scientists and machine engineers, to realizably build and deploy AI-enabled applications at scale.

In the 2024 edition of the State of AI in Financial Services Report, more than 80% of survey respondents reported that AI is driving increased revenue and reduced annual costs, with customer service, risk management, portfolio optimization, fraud detection, and intelligent document management being some of the AI use cases that companies are investing in today. Accelerated computing is delivering breakthrough performance in this next wave of AI, producing tokens of pieces of intelligence using data. Imagine generative AI co-pilots being able to leverage such vast amount of data that we have opted in to share via open banking and other platform technologies. As with co-pilots at work that can improve our productivity, these personal co-pilots can act as stewards of our financial journeys and guide us toward more secure financial future.

The opportunities to deliver the next level of differentiated financial products are vast. Banking has done amazing at taking new innovations from ATMs to the internet, mobile, and cloud. With AI, financial institutions can now build and deploy better processes and products at scale, capturing competitive advantage, reducing inefficiencies, and growing revenue through new technological platforms.

With improved accuracy of open-source large language models, new generative AI-powered digital avatars and digital humans will provide better customer service, deliver more personalized recommendations, and help customer service agents solve more complex problems faster.

Looking ahead, as we continue our journey, we must continue to keep energy efficiency in mind as we improve performance—not just from a chip level but also from a full software stack level. And to drive further economic development with AI, we need to train more workers and prepare tomorrow's workforce for future growth. We want more people to benefit and understand data science, generative AI, robotics, and quantum computing, so that they too can benefit from this new industrial revolution. As Bob Pette, NVIDIA's vice president and general manager of enterprise platforms said in his special address in the AI Summit in DC: "We will be doing an injustice if AI only helps a few. High tide raises all boats. We have to raise all boats."

Notes

1. Professor John McCarthy. Stanford University, n.d. jmc.stanford.edu/general/index.html.

2. OECD (2024), "Explanatory memorandum on the updated OECD definition of an AI system", OECD Artificial Intelligence Papers, No. 8, OECD Publishing, Paris, https://doi.org/10.1787/623da898-en.

3. Britannica, The Editors of Encyclopedia. "three laws of robotics". Encyclopedia Britannica, 13 May. 2024, https://www.britannica.com/topic/Three-Laws-of-Robotics. Accessed 3 June 2024.

4. Britannica, The Editors of Encyclopedia. "Turing test". Encyclopedia Britannica, 31 May. 2024, https://www.britannica.com/technology/Turing-test. Accessed 3 June 2024.

5. 75 Years of Innovation: Shakey the Robot. SRI. Nd. https://www.sri.com/press/story/75-years-of-innovation-shakey-the-robot/

6. Stanford HCI Group. "SHRDLU". nd. https://hci.stanford.edu/winograd/shrdlu/

7. https://www.youtube.com/watch?v=03p2CADwGF8

8. Britannica, The Editors of Encyclopaedia. "Chinese room argument". Encyclopedia Britannica, 5 Jun. 2024, https://www.britannica.com/topic/Chinese-room-argument. Accessed 6 June 2024.

9. J McDermott (1980). "R1: An Expert in the Computer Systems Domain" (PDF). Proceedings of the First AAAI Conference on Artificial Intelligence. AAAI'80. Stanford, California: AAAI Press: 269–271. https://cdn.aaai.org/AAAI/1980/AAAI80-076.pdf

10. https://cyc.com/leadership-team/

11. D Monroe. Seeking Artificial Common Sense, Communications of the ACM, Nov 1, 2020. https://cacm.acm.org/news/seeking-artificial-common-sense/

12. B.J Copeland. nouvelle artificial intelligence, Encyclopedia Britannica, 18 Sep. 2023, https://www.britannica.com/technology/nouvelle-artificial-intelligence. Accessed 7 June 2024.

13. A Pollack. 'Fifth Generation' became Japan's lost generation, New York Times, June 5, 1992. https://www.nytimes.com/1992/06/05/business/fifth-generation-became-japan-s-lost-generation.html

14. 25 years since the world's first text message, Vodafone, Dec 4, 2017. https://www.vodafone.com/news/technology/25-anniversary-text-message

15. Watson, 'Jeopardy!' champion. IBM, nd. https://www.ibm.com/history/watson-jeopardy

16. AlphaGo. Google DeepMind, n.d. https://deepmind.google/technologies/alphago/

17. AI Colonialism. MIT Technology Review, n.d. https://www.technologyreview.com/supertopic/ai-colonialism-supertopic

18. D Berreby. As Use of A.I. Soars, So Does the Energy and Water It Requires, YaleEnvironment360, February 6, 2024. https://e360.yale.edu/features/artificial-intelligence-climate-energy-emissions
19. The state of AI in early 2024: Gen AI adoption spikes and starts to generate value, McKinsey, May 30, 2024. https://www.mckinsey.com/capabilities/quantumblack/our-insights/the-state-of-ai
20. The state of AI Q2'24 Report, CB Insights, July 30, 2024. https://www.cbinsights.com/research/report/ai-trends-q2-2024/
21. G Marcus. What Facebook wants with artificial intelligence, The New Yorker, December 9, 2013. https://www.newyorker.com/tech/annals-of-technology/what-facebook-wants-with-artificial-intelligence
22. mRNA and Artificial Intelligence for Advanced Vaccine Innovation. Pfizer, n.d. https://www.pfizer.com/news/articles/how_a_novel_incubation_sandbox_helped_speed_up_data_analysis_in_pfizer_s_covid_19_vaccine_trial
23. Demis Hassabis & John Jumper awarded Nobel Prize in Chemistry, Google DeepMind, 9 October 2024. https://deepmind.google/discover/blog/demis-hassabis-john-jumper-awarded-nobel-prize-in-chemistry/
24. A global food crisis. World Food Programme, nd. https://www.wfp.org/global-hunger-crisis
25. S Barchenger, Your Waymo got pulled over. What happens next in Phoenix? Arizona Republic, 2 July 2024. https://www.azcentral.com/story/news/local/arizona/2024/07/02/what-happens-when-a-waymo-gets-pulled-over-in-phoenix/74197111007/
26. Y Shimbun, Japan's Transport Ministry Proposes Automated Logistics Link Between Tokyo and Osaka, The Japan News, 23 June 2024. https://japannews.yomiuri.co.jp/business/economy/20240623-193996/
27. Cargo Sous Terrain, n.d. https://www.cst.ch/en/the-project/
28. 2024 Consumer Study: Revolutionize retail with AI everywhere, IBM Institute for Business Value, January 5, 2024. https://www.ibm.com/thought-leadership/institute-business-value/en-us/report/ai-retail
29. M Yagoda, Airline held liable for its chatbot giving passenger bad advice—what this means for travellers, BBC, February 23, 2024 https://www.bbc.com/travel/article/20240222-air-canada-chatbot-misinformation-what-travellers-should-know
30. ChatGPT provides false information about people, and OpenAI can't correct it, noyb, April 29, 2024. https://noyb.eu/en/chatgpt-provides-false-information-about-people-and-openai-cant-correct-it

31. Weiser, Mark. Scientific American, The Computer for the twenty-first Century, Sept 1, 1991, https://www.scientificamerican.com/article/the-computer-for-the-21st-century/

2

The Rise of AI and Generative AI

AI is not magic.

The hype is real. AI is everywhere all around us—in our daily lives and in our workplaces, in earnings reports and on the news. According to data from Arize, 64.6% of US-based Fortune 500 companies mention AI in their most recent annual financial reports; over one in five specifically made a reference to generative AI.[1]

McKinsey wrote that generative AI's impact on productivity could add trillions of dollars in value to the global economy. Similarly, Goldman Sachs speculated that breakthroughs in generative AI could "drive a 7% (or almost $7 trillion) increase in global GDP and lift productivity growth by 1.5 percentage points over a 10-year period". Citibank wrote that AI could "potentially drive global banking industry profits to $2 trillion by 2028", representing a 9% increase over the next five years from 2024, excluding non-bank financial sector profits.[2]

Could this be over-optimism like what we have experienced in prior AI summers? Or is this driven by fear of missing out (FOMO)?

Some might call this an AI arms race, especially in the venture space. According to CB Insights data, AI start-ups raised $42.5 billion across 2500 equity rounds in 2023. Although generative AI represents only a small slice of the AI pie, from a technology perspective, it managed to capture 48% of all AI funding that same year.

What fuels the optimism, the explosive growth in interests, and the hype in this last cycle? Who are the players in the ecosystem and what role do they play in the evolving landscape (Fig. 2.1)?

© The Author(s), under exclusive license to Springer Nature
Switzerland AG 2025
T. Lau, *Banking on (Artificial) Intelligence*, https://doi.org/10.1007/978-3-031-81647-5_2

THE RISE OF AI
& GENERATIVE AI

- PRACTICAL USE CASES OF AI.

- THE PREDICTIONS: DO THESE NUMBERS EVEN MAKE SENSE?

GENERATIVE AI'S IMPACT ON PRODUCTIVITY COULD ADD TRILLIONS OF DOLLARS IN VALUE TO THE GLOBAL ECONOMY.

LIFT PRODUCTIVITY GROWTH BY 1.5 PERCENTAGE POINTS OVER A 10-YEAR PERIOD

BREAKTHROUGHS IN GENERATIVE AI COULD....

DRIVE A 7% (OR ALMOST $7 TRILLION) INCREASE IN GLOBAL GDP

WHAT FUELS OPTIMISM IN THIS LAST CYCLE?

- EXPLOSIVE GROWTH IN INTERESTS
- DATA
- COMPUTE

"AI ARMS RACE"

- WHO ARE THE PLAYERS IN THE ECOSYSTEM
- WHAT ROLE DO THEY PLAY IN THE EVOLVING LANDSCAPE?

STATE OF FUNDING

PARTNERSHIPS

Fig. 2.1 The rise of AI and Generative AI

Practical Use Cases of AI in Financial Services

According to Goldman Sachs, share of public companies mentioning AI on their earning calls in 2023 surged to 27.6% in the US and 30.4% in Europe, from 8.4% in the US and 7.2% in Europe just three years prior in 2020.[3]

This is hardly surprising, as not a day goes by without hearing something about AI. During one of my travels in early 2024, I overheard someone saying: "Give some of that Gen AI!" on a call at the airport. It reminded me of the saying: "Show me the money!".

While AI is not new, as we have explored in Chapter 1, adoption of AI within financial services has remained relatively steady in the past few years, especially when serving as smart assistants or copilots to employees' daily tasks. Interests exploded in late 2022 with the introduction of ChatGPT and other generative AI tools. But AI is more than just a chatbot—it can be a powerful tool for change, with benefits extended beyond what we can imagine.

Good news is, consumers are also becoming more receptive of AI being used in banking, with the caveat being that if they have visibility into how it is being used and can choose how it is being applied, according to GPT's Banking Disruption Index. Use cases around safeguarding consumers' financial assets and helping them with practical aspects of everyday banking such as checking balance and transferring funds are particularly welcomed.[4]

In this section, we will explore where AI has been deployed and where some of the more exciting opportunities lie. This is not meant to be an exhaustive list of all the applications of AI in financial services, but a representative one that will continue to evolve, along with use cases and input from industry experts.

Coding

At the front row seat of the future of financial services is technology. From upkeeping existing systems to meeting new business and regulatory requirements, AI, in particular generative AI, can help automate tasks, create new code, and perform Q&A. By using Microsoft's GitHub Copilot coding assistant to write software code, Goldman Sachs developers, for example, can build more applications faster, gaining about 20% increase in efficiency in the process.[5]

To illustrate how much the technology is progressing, Andy Jassy, President and CEO at Amazon, highlighted the capabilities of Amazon Q, Amazon's generative AI assistant for software development, in a LinkedIn post. The average time to upgrade an application to Java 17, for example, went down from 50 developer-days to a few hours, saving 4500 developer-years of work.[6] As a result, the Amazon Q team has been able to upgrade more than half of their production Java systems to modernized versions, introducing enhanced security and reduced infrastructure costs, with an estimated $260 million in annualized efficiency gains.

Looking toward the future, can AI be used to update legacy systems written in COBOL, a programming language developed in the 1950s and is still used in many core banking systems? According to IBM, the answer is a definite yes. In fact, the tech giant believes that modernizing mainframe applications is a crucial step in the digital transformation journey. In a case study shared, Westfield Insurance demonstrated 30% time savings by using a generative AI code assistant to sift through 47,000 lines of code in its mainframe environment and 80% time savings in application discovery analysis.[7] Since mainframe applications are often written in older programming languages (such as COBOL), organizations often face challenges when it comes to transforming the code to Java. Being able to use generative AI capabilities to solve for this is a true gamechanger.

Customer Service

Use of generative AI in customer service is gaining momentum. Through integration with Microsoft Teams and Dynamics 365, for example, call center tools can help identify new business opportunities and drive new revenue. Intelligent chatbots and virtual assistants can be leveraged to perform trend and sentiment analysis and empower agents to deliver service faster and more effectively through insights and recommended next best actions provided in real time. Generative AI can also be used to automatically generate contact summaries and analyze interactions, thus saving time and improving the quality of customer interactions, while providing records for training and compliance purposes.

Similar capabilities can be deployed outside the call centers and into the hands of consumers as well. Bunq, the second largest neobank based in Europe, with 11 million users across the EU, launched Finn, a generative AI platform for their users at the end of 2023. Finn is equipped with a chat-style text box where users can ask questions or seek advice about their bank account, spending habits, saving and anything else related to money. Such capabilities can prove useful as consumers increasingly seek self-service features that go above and beyond the traditional mechanisms.

But as we have witnessed so far, it can also be incredibly risky to use unvetted machine-generated language for external customer-facing applications, especially when it comes to matters of finance. Something that looks good in generated text does not necessary mean that it is entirely accurate or factual—especially as it lacks context. A more desirable and safer approach will be to leverage traditional language models to decipher the customer inquiries and then map them back to the pool of scripted answers in the repository to ensure that an accurate answer can be consistently provided.

Such is the approach undertaken by DBS when they deployed their in-house developed CSO Assistant. The tool transcribes the voice conversation between the customer service representative and the bank customer, then searches the bank's knowledge base to fetch and integrate information, in order to provide suggestions to the rep as a next step. And at the end of the call, the virtual assistant auto-generates a call summary.

The CSO Assistant is expected to reduce call handling time by up to 20%, according to DBS' press release, based on data collected since the pilots began in October 2023. Most notably, the virtual assistant has demonstrated nearly 100% accuracy when it comes to transcription and solutioning.[8] This is crucial especially for financial services industry, where trust and accuracy are paramount.

The case of Air Canada's chatbot giving the wrong information to a passenger serves as a cautionary tale on what could go wrong with generative AI chatbots when humans are not in the loop. The airline was ordered by the Civil Resolution Tribunal in Canada to compensate the passenger for damages caused since the chatbot provided the wrong information on bereavement fare to the passenger on Air Canada's website.[9] What was remarkable with this case was that the airline initially argued that the chatbot was a separate legal entity responsible for their own actions.[10]

Despite potential risks for mishaps, however, it is not surprising that customer-focused use cases such as creating human-like chatbots are top priorities for many organizations. Done properly, such efforts can help drive significant cost savings through operational efficiency improvement, especially for smaller institutions.

Spotlight on Casca
Based on conversation with Lukas Haffer, CEO of Casca.

Loan application processes are stressful and cumbersome. For smaller banks, the underwriting for small business loans often proves to be so intensive that the effort may not be worth the time. But what if we can use technology to facilitate the loan file preparation so that banks can originate more loans and small business owners can get faster access to the credit that they need?

Such was the quest that Casca embarked on with a community bank based in Connecticut, and the results have been promising. According to Lukas, the conversion rate using the AI assistant, Sarah, has increased dramatically to over 80%. Having Sarah embedded as part of the online loan application process provides an opportunity for the virtual assistant to step in proactively to help whenever the applicant runs into any roadblocks at any given point in time. Inquiries can now be resolved right away, instead of waiting for when the loan officer is available during regular bank hours.

As it turns out, the busiest time for Sarah tends to be on Friday evenings, when the small business owners can afford the time to get the paperwork done. Traditionally, it is also the time when the banks are closed, and no one is available to answer any questions that the loan applicants may have. With Sarah deployed, loan files can now be completed around the clock and ready for review and final approval in a much shorter timeframe. Separately, Sarah can also help to reactive churned applications, while saving 90% of manual effort in document collection.

"How does a bespoke private banker experience look like? And how can we offer that to more small businesses by leveraging technology?"

Casca's partnership with the community bank serves as a great example of how banks and fintechs can partner to make banking magical. And the fintech is just getting started.

Expense Management

Remember the envelopes full of paper receipts? Now there is an AI for that. Take SAP Concur as an example. Through their partnership with Mastercard, the business travelers can now have their purchases made via the Mastercard corporate cards automatically captured and populated in the Concur Expense platform. The system will also alert the users right away if further actions are required. Beyond providing a better user experience, such automated expense creation capabilities can help to improve cost control and policy compliance, through streamlining operations to reduce manual tasks and errors.

Gone are the days that we need to manually enter the receipt amount, date, location, and expense type, as the AI model can do that for us now when we upload the receipt.

Can we envision one day where the expense process that can practically manage itself? After all, dealing with expense reports and waiting to get reimbursed is probably the least enjoyable part of any business travel.

Fraud

Concerns around cybersecurity and fraud are nothing new. After all, bad actors go where the money is. Rapid development in AI has drastically lowered the point of entry for scammers as it is now easier than ever to create and spread deepfake content to larger group of unsuspecting victims, using personal information that make the scams seem even more realistic and convincing, or impersonating tactics to convince people that they are sending money to a legitimate entity. Gone are the days of phishing emails and website content with typos, one of the typical signs to watch for. According to ACI Worldwide and GlobalData, authorized push payment (APP) fraud losses are expected to reach $5.25 billion across the US, UK, and India by 2026, with the most common being product, romance, and investment scams.[11]

While AI has always played a significant role in monitoring for potential financial crimes and fraud, as AI development continues to progress, using AI to fight AI crimes is fast becoming an area of great interest. Mastercard, for example, has leveraged their AI-powered cybersecurity solutions to combat real-time payment scams, and they have managed to stop over $35 billion in fraud losses in the past three years.[12]

Prevention and monitoring remain key in fraud prevention. Many of these tools can monitor network traffic in real time, alerting security teams of any suspicious activities detected. And since these systems can continue to evolve and learn, they can be used to fight against new threats as well. Such a method also makes commercial sense. According to the IBM study, Cost of the Data Breach Report, the average total cost of a data breach jumped 10% from $4.45 million in 2023 to $4.88 million in 2024; but organizations can save $2.2 million on average in breach costs when AI is deployed extensively in prevention.[13]

But cybersecurity has always been an evolving cat-and-mouse game between criminals and defenders. Although AI is being used to detect anomalies and create better defenses against malicious acts, hackers are also leveraging the technology to create more intelligent malware and automate their attacks. Credential stuffing attacks is one such example, where credential lists can be automatically created by combining stolen credentials and data dumps from multiple sources (e.g. data breaches), enabling attacks to be done at a much larger scale with increased frequency.

With advanced generative AI tools, scammers can now impersonate high-profile personalities to demand payments. In one such case, a finance worker was tricked into believing that he was attending a video conference with his company's chief financial officer, who asked to have $25.6 million remitted. As it turned out, the CFO in the video conference, along with other people, were created using deepfake technology.[14]

While humans are generally considered to be the weakest link when it comes to cybersecurity, the complexity level of tools available for fraudsters has made it more challenging to spot malicious attempts. With increasingly sophisticated technology that can create facial expressions and accents that seem *natural*, it may become harder to detect deepfakes and assess if the *person* you are talking to is indeed real. Fake identities can be created using computer-generated faces to bypass traditional identity verification process. Social engineering scams are increasingly being used to target specific individuals via networking sites such as LinkedIn.

It is perhaps no wonder that Gartner predicts that by 2026, 30% of enterprises will no longer rely solely on identity verification and authentication solutions due to the prevalence of AI-generated deepfakes.[15]

Beyond leveraging mechanisms such as liveness detection, location intelligence, and behavioral analytics, organizations must ensure that they have the proper processes and procedures in place, including training for employees and education for customers. Creating an effective cyber defense mechanism is akin to peeling an onion; as technology is evolving at a fast pace, a multi-layer strategy that includes both humans and AI is prudent.

According to the FTC, a record $10 billion has been reported lost to scams in 2023 nationwide, up from $9 billion the year prior. However, since most victims do not report their losses, the actual amount is likely much higher.[16] And most consumers reported having experienced fraud at least once, according to a survey conducted by SAS, "Faces of Fraud: Consumer Experiences With Fraud and What It Means for Businesses": Nearly half indicated that they have experienced more fraud in 2022 compared to prior years, and most consumers are becoming more wary of fraud.[17]

Given the prevalence of fraud, service providers have more to lose, beyond financial and reputational risks. According to the same SAS survey, nine in 10 consumers believe that organizations should be doing more to protect them from fraud, and that two-thirds of the consumers indicated that they would switch providers due to fraud or if another provider offered better fraud protections. The research revealed that most customers are willing to sacrifice some convenience for stronger safeguards, including "accepting more checks and delays in transactions". Interestingly, that's the approach that fintech Charlie is taking. Charlie is a fintech targeting the older demographics. When a new payee or a device that has not been used in 30 days is added to an account, or if the transfer is higher than $100, its anti-fraud feature, called SpeedBump, will pause the payment transaction for up to six hours to notify the account holder.[18]

We will go deeper into the world of risk management and fraud in later part of the book.

Compliance

One of the greatest strengths of AI is the ability to quickly and effectively analyze a vast amount of data, which makes it well-suited for tasks that require deciphering pages of documents (e.g. regulatory guidance and earnings reports) to summarize and generate insights for stakeholders. This is particularly useful when it comes to handling large amount of unstructured data such as press release, corporate disclosures, call transcripts, and videos. Given the mundane nature of the task, this is easily one of the areas ripe for automation that can bring about increased productivity.

Citi, for example, already leverages generative AI to prepare new projects for compliance review by creating project summaries and determining which regulations would apply. This enables organizations to adapt to changes in regulatory requirements and focus the compliance team's efforts on areas that require more detailed assessment, saving valuable time and resources.[19]

Internal Copilot

One of the more common use cases on generative AI centers around automating information gathering. With Amazon Q, for example, employees can find information within the digital walls of the enterprise, generate content, and gain insights; the interactions can be configured based on each individual user's identity, role, and level of access. With simple prompts, the AI assistant can draft e-mails based on a press release, write an article, summarize a report, and so on.

AI summaries are becoming more commonplace with other tools as well. Collaboration platform, Webex, for example, automatically captures important action items and creates meeting summaries with AI for Webex conference meetings. ChatGPT can be used to summarize and provide a list of links to internal documents based on the user search criteria.

In the 2024 I/O developer conference event, Google unveiled its plan to roll out AI-generated search summary by the end of 2024. From searching using a simple box and keywords to present day, where we can search by capturing a video, or having a full trip itinerary created based on one query, we have come a long way.

Such a pragmatic step-by-step approach can be seen as JPMorgan Chase embarks on the generative AI journey. While the bank has been working with AI for many years on areas such as fraud prevention, deploying generative AI solutions is a relatively new endeavor. The initial rollout included providing the generative AI assistant to the bank's more than 60,000 employees, to help with drafting emails, summarizing reports, and generative ideas.[20] It is envisioned that the next phase will involve infusing the models with proprietary bank data for productivity gains. And the final phase will enable AI agents to perform more complex operations autonomously.

Lending

One of the most fascinating use cases in AI lending that I have come across to-date is the "310 lending model" employed by MYbank, a digital bank under the Ant Group umbrella. Using the mobile app, small business owners can apply for a collateral-free business loan in three minutes, get approved within one second, and with no human interaction.

This data-driven approach to lending is touted as a more effective mechanism to provide much needed capital to micro, small, and medium enterprise (MSMEs), compared to traditional credit scoring, as many of MYbank's new customers were first-time borrowers. The risks are minimized by using algorithms to assess monthly sales and repayment patterns of the small business.[21] With MSMEs facing a finance gap of 43% in China (and higher elsewhere),[22] there is much to be gained not only by organizations that leverage the power of data and AI to close the gap, but for the whole economy.

According to MYbank's 2023 Annual Report, the bank has served 53 million MSMEs as of the end of 2023, all without the need for physical branches.[23] This helps to extend funding to businesses at moments of emergency, as well as capital to expand and grow.

In the meantime, however, care must be taken to ensure that the outcome of the automated lending decisions can be explained. In the US for example, the CFPB (Consumer Financial Protection Bureau) has stated in numerous occasions that financial institutions must be able to explain how credit decisions are made, regardless of the complexity and novelty of the technology. And that "robust fair lending testing of models should include regular testing for disparate treatment and disparate impact, including searches for and implementation of less discriminatory alternatives using manual or automated techniques".[24]

In other words, no black box.

At the time of writing this chapter, the Consumer Federation of America and Consumer Reports sent a letter to the CFPB, urging the agency to set ground rules for the use of algorithmic decision-making tools.[25] The letter pressed for regulatory clarity on the need to search for and implement less discriminatory alternatives when using the algorithms for credit underwriting and pricing, to reduce risk of harm to consumers. We will explore this further throughout the book as this is an important topic that is still evolving.

Investing

With the volume of data and types of data in the market that can influence investment strategies, AI acts as a great copilot that can sort through the data and locate trends and patterns to help humans make more informed investment decisions. This is especially crucial considering that an overwhelming majority of the world's data is unstructured, in the form of streaming video and audio, news articles, social media posts, online forums, PDFs, and more. The ability to go beyond traditional news analytics to gauge investor sentiment is crucial in uncovering potential signals of market shifts and risks in a timely and effective manner is a key competitive advantage.

With generative AI, we are now beginning to see AI chatbot applications that offer recommendations for retail investing. Bridgewise, a Tel Aviv-based AI startup, has received approval from the Israel Securities Authority to launch Bridget, where investors can ask for buy and sell recommendations on stocks.[26] Future updates will include share price forecasts, earning call transcripts, and thematic portfolios. This is quite a significant milestone for generative AI, where it has mostly been used for research and customer service.

Wealth Management

With consumers becoming increasingly comfortable with using digital tools to manage various aspects of their daily lives, it is inevitable that the wealth management industry needs to adapt to the changing habits as well. We are at an interesting crossroad where the industry is serving four, to perhaps even five, generations of investors at the same time, with varied needs, preferences, and lived experiences. As social media enables better access to financial information and education, breaking down the barrier of entry to investing, especially to the younger investors and those who are underrepresented, a growing number of people have become more open to receiving AI-generated financial advice, upending an industry that relies heavily on the human touch.

Betterment and Wealthfront are two of the earlier platforms that offer fully automated robo-advisory services and are intended to provide more affordable ways to invest for ordinary people with less assets. Beyond an entry-level service with automatic portfolio rebalancing, some of these firms, including WealthSimple, one of Canada's first robo-advisor, also offer a different tier for wealthier clients who want access to dedicated wealth advisors.

While we may not yet see wealth advisors being fully replaced by AI, there are still many ways that technology acts as copilots for humans, from providing predictive insights to optimizing investment portfolio and assisting with client engagement. For instance, rather than human advisors conducting manual searches, AI can be used to automate analysis of historical data, social media content, news, analyst reports, and corporate earnings call transcripts, identifying market trends and changes in market sentiments, and uncovering crucial insights and opportunities to help advisors make more informed data-driven decisions. Wealth managers from UBS and HSBC, for example, have been using AI to analyze market data, assess risk, and tailor investment strategies for their clients, streamlining the amount of time it would take on market research and synthesize data.

Meanwhile, for self-service, Charles Schwab's virtual Schwab Assistant digital tool leverages natural language processing capabilities to analyze customer inquiries and guide them toward the information that they are looking for. The tool can also create a summary of the chat conversation while referring the customer to a human representative, thus streamlining the end-to-end experience. Recently, Morgan Stanley has also started experimenting with generative AI to help with client meetings, summarizing the discussions, surfacing action items, and drafting initial communications.

While AI may not replace our jobs, those who know how to leverage AI tools to do the jobs will gain a competitive edge compared to those who don't.

The Fuel Behind the Latest AI Boom

The latest round of AI optimism started with the launch of ChatGPT in November 2022. Not to be outdone by OpenAI, big tech companies have been racing to get new generative AI tools out to market, including Claude by Anthropic, Copilot by Microsoft, Gemini by Google, and Imagine by Meta. Separately, OpenAI has also released its text-to-video generative AI tool in early 2024.

Interestingly, in their Worldwide Developer Conference (WWDC) in June 2024, Apple forged a slightly different path. Rather than pursuing the OpenAI tactics in a jaw-dropping way that some critics have compared to the movie "Her", Apple coins their generative AI technology "Apple Intelligence", focusing on creating personalized experience and infusing productivity in its suite of products with generative AI. The company calls it "AI for the rest of us".[27]

As much as AI seems to be progressing at lightning speed in the past two years, it is helpful to remember that the progress of human civilization does not happen overnight. Rather it relies on knowledge and experience that has been accumulated for centuries. The same can be said about technology and the progress of innovation. The journey of AI development has not always been an easy path. Looking back, it may be hard to believe that we have already experienced two AI winters. From the initial excitement prompted by SHRDLU—thought to be a breakthrough moment for AI to be able to understand the English language, along with Shakey the Robot, which laid the foundation of today's self-driving vehicles, to where we are today. While we have come a long way, numerous hurdles will remain with AI in the real world.

I'd like to think of technology innovation as Lego blocks—with one brick building on top of the other. We can create different structures based on our imagination; and we can also take them apart and re-create something new. Just as how Clippy preceded the conversational agents that we have today, and how Shakey the robot was the first general-purpose mobile robot with enough AI to navigate on its own in the early 70 s—long before NASA's exploration Mars Rovers, or the autonomous vehicles that descend onto the streets of San Francisco and Arizona in present day. And even Shakey, built by the Stanford Research Institute, was constructed using component technologies that existed: TV camera, radio communications, range finder, and a set of drive wheels with stepping motors.[28] When the first working image dissector was tested by Philo Farnsworth in 1927, I doubt that anyone would have thought it would be used to guide a *robot* one day. And beyond self-driving cars, robot vacuum cleaners, and GPS for navigation, Shakey has helped inspire different systems that we use today, including Siri, with its natural language interactions. It now rests at the Computer History Museum in Mountain View, California.

The success of the innovations that we experience today rests on the shoulders of technology advances and failures from decades before. While we might not have all the answers right away as we continue our AI journey, it is helpful to remember to take the long view on innovation.

The Predictions

A quick look at the sheer number of reports produced on a particular topic gives us a sense of where the world is heading and where the attention—hence the money—goes. The most challenging part about writing this book is to keep up with the changes with such a fast-evolving topic. This is especially true when it comes to predictions on the economic potential and impact of the technology.

From private sector to policymakers and academia, one thing remains certain, however. Even though the jury is still out when it comes to the true economic potential of generative AI, for example, cautious optimism abounds.

Do These Numbers Even Make Sense?

By far, Goldman Sachs seems to be one of the bold ones. Back in 2023, the Wall Street firm wrote that breakthroughs in generative AI could "drive a 7% (or almost $7 trillion) increase in global GDP and lift productivity growth by 1.5 percentage points over a 10-year period".[29] The firm also predicted in the same research that around the world, "shifts in workflows triggered by these advances could expose the equivalent of 300 million full-time jobs to automation".

Interestingly, a subsequent brief from Goldman Sachs, struck a different tone.

"AI's potential productivity impacts do not matter if the enabling economic and legal environment cannot be put in place to take advantage of it—the AI transition relies on more than just the AI innovators."

Building out the AI infrastructure is costly; it is inevitably a journey that can be undertaken only by those with resources. But using AI to replace the lower-age tasks is akin to using a Lamborghini to deliver pizza—an analogy that I learned from a WSJ article a while back that stuck with me.

Though Goldman Sachs is hardly alone with bold predictions. IBM, for instance, shared in their 2024 Global Outlook for Banking and Financial Markets, that "8 in 10 institutions is tactically implementing generative AI for at least one use case". Meanwhile, Citibank estimated that AI could add $170 billion (9%), from $1.7 billion to $2 billion, to the global banks sector profit pool by 2028.[30]

The hype undoubtedly fueled the excitement behind startups such as OpenAI, which hoped to raise $6.5 billion with a valuation of $150 billion.[31]

But what trillion-dollar problem will AI be able to solve to make the investment worthwhile? And will our society be ready to adapt—given the resource-intensive operations, the regulatory environment, and the talent gap?

The interesting thing about predictions is that they are still, just predictions. Trying to guestimate the outcome of AI is immensely difficult. First and foremost, who the technology will impact the most—and how—is still a great unknown. While AI will likely have an impact on anything that can be automated (i.e. both service-level tasks as well as white-collar jobs), the extent of the impact (i.e. adoption) and what comes after that is less than certain. Will the displaced workers be retrained/upskilled to do something different? Will the new jobs be more stable or still as prone to disruption by AI or other advanced technologies? How will the change impact the younger generation and their earning power? Given the demand for those skilled in AI amongst all the verticals, from private sector and government to higher institutions, we will most likely face a talent constraint. How will competition for talent impact different local economies and the AI hotspots such as San Francisco and Montreal?

And let's not forget the industries that will be impacted by it. Supporting the sea change will require more data centers and digital infrastructure to be built, which are likely in more rural areas. This will trigger ripple effects on the local economies, including but not limited to increased demand for services such as maintenance and security, in addition to auxiliary jobs to support building out the facilities. Will this balance out some of the benefits that coastal cities will gain? How will the rivalry between countries and regions impact the collective gains and distribution of benefits?

While we may not be able to pinpoint the net economic outcome from AI, this much is likely true: The future will be favorable to those who can leverage AI.

How are organizations seizing the opportunity now, and more importantly, what should we keep in mind as we progress? The consulting giant, McKinsey, offered the following in their report titled: "The state of AI in early 2024"[32]:

- 65% of organizations are using AI on a regular basis, which is nearly double the percentage from the previous McKinsey Global Survey only 10 months ago.
- 44% of respondents say their organization has already experienced negative consequences from generative AI use, including inaccuracy in outputs, cybersecurity and lack of explainability. Other issues include incorrect use of AI and data privacy, bias or intellectual property infringement.
- Some companies report insufficient amounts of training data, a struggle to define processes for data governance and quick integration of data.
- Just 18% of respondents said their employers had an enterprise-wide council or board focused on responsible AI governance.

As more organizations who have embarked on the generative AI journey have discovered, significant handholding is still needed to make the tool work. Having a solid data strategy—keeping data organized and updated—is a key first step.

While we continue to be fascinated by what technology can help us achieve, we must not lose sight of potential challenges that we must address, including bias, ethics, data privacy and security, governance, as well as job displacement, competition, and resource needs.

We will explore each of these topics in further details throughout the book.

AI is Not Magic

As much as AI may feel magical or even intelligent at times, nothing brings us back to reality than a story that shows how human this really is.

Take Amazon's Just Walk Out technology as an example. I remember shopping at one of the Whole Foods Market locations that was beta testing the technology before the official rollout. It felt surreal to be able to just take anything off the shelf and walk out of the store with a digital receipt tallying all the items. I also felt a sense of unease with all the cameras that were mounted on the ceiling and sensors on the shelves, watching our every move. I remember remarking to the kids that I felt like we were being followed. I was also concerned about data privacy and what Amazon would do with all the data from the cameras and sensors. Nevertheless, I was intrigued and wondered if this would be the future of grocery shopping: Cashierless, checkout-free, and devoid of human connections.

Fast forward to 2024 and Amazon announced that they are dropping Just Walk Out from its US Amazon Fresh grocery stores and switching to Amazon's Dash Cart, which automatically tallies up the items as you shop. At the same time, Amazon refuted a claim that the technology needed as many as 700 human reviewers for every 1000 customer transactions.[33] In a company blog post, Dilip Kumar, Vice President of AWS Applications, clarified that while the Amazon associates were responsible for labeling and annotating data, "this is no different than any other AI system that places a high value on accuracy, where human reviewers are common."[34]

The story reminds me of another AI hype in 2014 with x.ai, a startup that claimed to be an AI personal assistant in the name of "Amy" who could schedule meetings and email appointments for you using natural language. Unfortunately, as it turned out, behind the "artificial" part of the "artificial intelligence" bots were real humans.[35]

Whether it is humans pretending to be machines or machines pretending to be humans—which one would you choose? This is of course not to dismiss nor minimize the potential of the technology, as we have only begun to surface what is possible. However, it does serve as a reality check that we need to be mindful of the potential of AI washing, and the harm that it can potentially cost, including loss of trust by the public.

Spotlight on Penny Crosman, Executive Editor, Technology at American Banker

When I decided to work on my third and current book, Penny Crosman was one of the first people that I thought of before I penned my first word. My first fintech interview was with Penny, who invited me to join her on American Banker podcast to talk about the innovation work that I was doing at the non-profit. And throughout the years, I have learned so much from Penny's writing and the way she articulates the stories.

Here is an excerpt of our conversation on where AI is heading for our industry.

Traditional forms of AI, like machine learning, have been used in banks for years, for things like detecting fraud and spotting cybersecurity intrusions. AI is very good at analyzing large swathes of data and finding potential red flags. Then an employee needs to investigate and determine if an anomaly is truly a sign of an intrusion or scam, or simply someone changing up their routine. These kinds of tried-and-true AI use cases are a good place to start. Most banks are dependent on their core vendors for integration help. In many cases, they will need to wait for their core provider to integrate with an AI system before they can use it.

When it comes to generative AI, I think banks need to tread very carefully and do small pilots. A lot can go wrong with this technology. One example of a misstep in this category is the case of Air Canada. Few banks are giving generative AI chatbots to customers due to the risks. But many are providing generative AI models to employees and encouraging them to use them in everyday tasks. JPMorgan Chase has said it plans to roll out an AI engine from OpenAI to all 240,000 employees and invite them to use it for drafting emails and reports. There haven't been public cases of such AI "copilots" causing harm. But they could feed employees misinformation. They could also stifle new ideas and fresh solutions to problems.

A lot of banks are experimenting with using generative AI to summarize calls in the contact center. As long as decisions aren't being made based on these automated transcripts, this seems like a use case that can save customer service reps a lot of time. Citi is rolling out generative AI to all its developers to help them build software using existing code from the bank's archive. If there truly is an adherence to repurposing Citi's own code, and the newly developed software is properly tested, this could save many hours of coding time. I think generative AI could also be useful at finding information in large troves of documents, with the ability to cite the original source turned on.

When it comes to regulations, so far, the bank regulators have only said that banks need to comply with all existing banking laws when they use AI in credit decisions, e.g. the Equal Credit Opportunity Act. But if regulators find that a bank or fintech has used AI to make loan decisions that break an existing law – for instance, if a bank's AI-based lending decisions are found to discriminate against a protected group – then the regulators are likely to impose more specific rules on banks and their vendors in this area.

To build trust, financial institutions need to conduct a lot of rigorous testing and monitoring. They can also build in guardrails and "human in the loop" checks. For instance, if a set of transactions fits a familiar fraud pattern, they can be sent to a human analyst to investigate. In cases like these, where the AI is doing research but not making actual decisions, I think trust can be formed.

When it comes to detecting payment fraud, banks could be doing more. If a customer has never wired money out of their account in 40 years, and suddenly they are wiring large sums to entities they've never sent money to before, that should be a red flag that should get further attention, for instance.

I also think banks need to have more staff dedicated to investigating fraud cases. Banks seem to be reluctant to devote time and resources to something that does not make them money. But there is cost—reputational risk and customer attrition risk—to being too quick to dismiss fraud claims.

Are we in an AI hype cycle or is this real? I think both are true. There is tremendous hype, and it is bound to die down. Yet the advances in AI are real. Personally, I don't expect to see banks adopt generative AI throughout their organizations. But I do think more traditional forms of AI are here to stay and they will continue to be deployed throughout the industry.

Notes

1. The rise of generative AI in SEC filings, Arize, July 2024. https://arize.com/wp-content/uploads/2024/07/The-Rise-of-Generative-AI-In-SEC-Filings-Arize-AI-Report-2024.pdf
2. AI in Finance, Citi, 17 June 2024. https://www.citigroup.com/global/insights/citigps/ai-in-finance
3. AI is showing 'very positive' signs of eventually boosting GDP and productivity. Goldman Sachs, 13 May 2024. https://www.goldmansachs.com/intelligence/pages/AI-is-showing-very-positive-signs-of-boosting-gdp.html
4. GFT U.S. Banking Disruption Index, GFT, 13 June 2024. https://www.gft.com/us/en/news/press-and-news/2024/press-releases/gft-usa-banking-disruption-index
5. I Bousquette, Goldman Sachs Deploys Its First Generative AI Tool Across the Firm, The Wall Street Journal, 27 June 2024. https://www.wsj.com/articles/goldman-sachs-deploys-its-first-generative-ai-tool-across-the-firm-cd94369b
6. Andy Jassy, August 2024. https://www.linkedin.com/posts/andy-jassy-8b1615_one-of-the-most-tedious-but-critical-tasks-activity-7232374162185461760-AdSz?utm_source=share&utm_medium=member_desktop
7. Mainframes as mainstays of digital transformation, IBM, 8 October 2024. https://www.ibm.com/thought-leadership/institute-business-value/en-us/report/mainframe-hybrid-cloud

8. DBS empowers its Customer Service Officers with Gen AI-powered virtual assistant to reduce toil and enhance customer experience, DBS, 18 July 2024. https://www.dbs.com/newsroom/DBS_empowers_its_Customer_Service_Officers_with_Gen_AI_powered_virtual_assistant_to_reduce_toil_and_enhance_customer_experience

9. https://bc.ctvnews.ca/air-canada-s-chatbot-gave-a-b-c-man-the-wrong-information-now-the-airline-has-to-pay-for-the-mistake-1.6769454

10. https://bc.ctvnews.ca/air-canada-s-chatbot-gave-a-b-c-man-the-wrong-information-now-the-airline-has-to-pay-for-the-mistake-1.6769454

11. Growth in APP Scams Expected To Double by 2026 – Report by ACI Worldwide and GlobalData, ACI Worldwide, 15 November 2022. https://www.businesswire.com/news/home/20221114006127/en/5327202/Growth-in-APP-Scams-Expected-To-Double-by-2026-%25E2%2580%2593-Report-by-ACI-Worldwide-and-GlobalData

12. Mastercard leverages its AI capabilities to fight real-time payment scams, Mastercard, 6 July 2024. https://www.mastercard.com/news/press/2023/july/mastercard-leverages-its-ai-capabilities-to-fight-real-time-payment-scams/

13. IBM, Cost of a Data Breach Report 2024, n.d. https://www.ibm.com/downloads/cas/1KZ3XE9D

14. H Chen and K Magramo, Finance worker pays out $25 million after video call with deepfake 'chief financial officer', CNN, 4 February, 2024. https://edition.cnn.com/2024/02/04/asia/deepfake-cfo-scam-hong-kong-intl-hnk/index.html

15. S Choubey, Gartner Predicts 30% of Enterprises Will Consider Identity Verification and Authentication Solutions Unreliable in Isolation Due to AI-Generated Deepfakes by 2026, Gartner, 1 February 2024. https://www.gartner.com/en/newsroom/press-releases/2024-02-01-gartner-predicts-30-percent-of-enterprises-will-consider-identity-verification-and-authentication-solutions-unreliable-in-isolation-due-to-deepfakes-by-2026

16. As Nationwide Fraud Losses Top $10 Billion in 2023, FTC Steps Up Efforts to Protect the Public, Federal Trade Commission, 9 February 2024. https://www.ftc.gov/news-events/news/press-releases/2024/02/nationwide-fraud-losses-top-10-billion-2023-ftc-steps-efforts-protect-public

17. Faces of Fraud, SAS, n.d. https://www.sas.com/en/whitepapers/faces-of-fraud-113582.html

18. S Gupta, This banking fintech for older Americans is launching a new feature to fight AI fraud, Fast Company, 24 June 2024. https://www.fastcompany.com/91143643/charlie-financial-fintech-older-people-ai-fraud-service

19. P Crosman, Why Citi is rolling out generative AI to all its developers, American Banker, 27 February 2024. https://www.americanbanker.com/news/why-citi-is-rolling-out-generative-ai-to-all-its-developers

20. H Son, JPMorgan Chase is giving its employees an AI assistant powered by ChatGPT maker OpenAI, CNBC, 9 August 2024. https://www.cnbc.com/2024/08/09/jpmorgan-chase-ai-artificial-intelligence-assistant-chatgpt-openai.html

21. MYBank's gender-driven approach to lending, IFC, August 2020. https://www.ifc.org/content/dam/ifc/doc/mgrt-pub/202008-d2e-mybank.pdf

22. SME Finance Forum, n.d. https://www.smefinanceforum.org/data-sites/msme-finance-gap#field-data-sites-tabs-tab-1

23. Leveraging AI, MYbank Enables Financing Services for 53 Million SMEs, Ant Group, 30 April 2024. https://www.antgroup.com/en/news-media/press-releases/1714473000000

24. Fair Lending Report of the Consumer Financial Protection Bureau, CFPB, June 2024, https://files.consumerfinance.gov/f/documents/cfpb_fair-lending-report_fy-2023.pdf

25. J Chen, Consumer groups' letter urging CFPB to protect consumers from discriminatory algorithms used by banks for making credit decisions, Consumer Reports, 26 June 2024, https://advocacy.consumerreports.org/research/consumer-groups-letter-urging-cfpb-to-protect-consumers-from-discriminatory-algorithms/

26. AI chatbot gets green light to give buy, sell investment advice, Bloomberg, 24 September 2024. https://www.investmentnews.com/fintech/ai-chatbot-gets-green-light-to-give-buy-sell-investment-advice/257373

27. Apple Intelligence, Apple, n.d. https://www.apple.com/apple-intelligence/

28. DARPA, Shakey the Robot, https://www.darpa.mil/about-us/timeline/shakey-the-robot

29. Generative AI could raise global GDP by 7%, Goldman Sachs, 5 April 2023. https://www.goldmansachs.com/intelligence/pages/generative-ai-could-raise-global-gdp-by-7-percent.html

30. AI in finance, Citibank, Citibank, 17 June 2024. https://www.citigroup.com/global/insights/citigps/ai-in-finance-bank-to-the-future

31. C Metz, M Isaac, T Mickle, and M de la Merced, OpenAI's Fund-Raising Talks Could Value Company at $150 Billion, New York Times, 11 September 2024. https://www.nytimes.com/2024/09/11/technology/openai-fund-raising-valuation.html

32. A Singla, A Sukharevsky, L Yee, M Chui, and B Hall, The state of AI in early 2024: Gen AI adoption spikes and.
    starts to generate value McKinsey, May 2024. https://www.mckinsey.com/capabilities/quantumblack/our-insights/the-state-of-ai

33. B Contreras. A Brief History of Automatons That Were Actually People, Scientific American, April 23, 2024. https://www.scientificamerican.com/article/is-there-a-human-hiding-behind-that-robot-or-ai/

34. D Kumar. An update on Amazon's plans for Just Walk Out and checkout-free technology, Amazon, April 17, 2024. https://www.aboutamazon.com/news/retail/amazon-just-walk-out-dash-cart-grocery-shopping-checkout-stores

35. E Huet. The Humans Hiding Behind the Chatbots, Bloomberg, April 18, 2016. https://www.bloomberg.com/news/articles/2016-04-18/the-humans-hiding-behind-the-chatbots

3

The Key Pillars of Responsible AI

Just because we can, doesn't mean we should.

While AI, especially generative AI, is often associated with chatbots and digital arts tools, the reality is, AI is much more than that. In this chapter, we will review the key pillars and importance of responsible innovation, including the humans behind the AI and the systemic biases that can influence the technology. The only challenge? It is impossible to anticipate and design for every scenario where the technology could be misused and exploited. And whose responsibility is it in the end, when the stakes can be so high and there are so many parties involved?

I wrote the majority of the first three chapters in Asia, where I was embedded in the energy and passion that drove the local innovation ecosystems. The growing regional divide was also becoming clearer as time went on, with OpenAI and Anthropic blocking access to their generative AI chatbots from Hong Kong, Macau, and China.

This signals a departure from the open access that Hong Kong has always enjoyed in the digital realm—without restrictions; it also serves as a reminder of the deepening tech war between the world's superpowers.

As I was strolling down Peel Street, a historic part of Central that locals cited as a living testament to the rich heritage in the ever-evolving city, I saw people going on with their daily lives: the small shop owner selling fresh fruits at a street corner, the trendy restaurant filling up with guests enjoying an evening out, and young people posing for selfies in front of the murals.

© The Author(s), under exclusive license to Springer Nature Switzerland AG 2025
T. Lau, *Banking on (Artificial) Intelligence*, https://doi.org/10.1007/978-3-031-81647-5_3

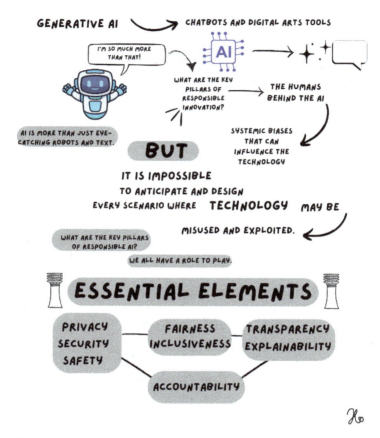

Fig. 3.1 The key pillars of responsible AI

It is impossible to predict the future trajectory of fast-developing technologies such as AI. But as we continue to explore the unchartered territories, I am reminded of something that I have always held true: Technology is a means to an end. Artificial intelligence, as a technology, is intended to benefit all of humanity, the ordinary people, in all corners of the earth. To harness its immense potential, we need collaboration, not isolation and division. Just as we need diverse data and collective brainpower to tackle the most difficult challenges.

Will we get there? Or will we repeat mistakes of the past, where power is concentrated in the hands of a few? And what can we do, as individuals, to bring more cohesion and harmony in the society (Fig. 3.1)?

What is Responsible AI?

The term *Responsible AI* has been mentioned so often, especially in corporate messaging, that you might be led to believe that it is something that has been embedded in our daily lives for a long time. Interestingly, a search on Google Trends would reveal that this is something rather new—with interest in the term skyrocketing after the launch of ChatGPT in late 2022 (Fig. 3.2).

But what exactly is responsible AI?

To embark on my discovery journey, I prompted a few of the prominent AI chatbots, including Microsoft Copilot, OpenAI ChatGPT, Anthropic Claude 3.5 Sonnet, Google Gemini, and Perplexity AI with the following: "What is responsible AI?".

Here is a sample of the response according to Perplexity AI.

Responsible AI is an approach to developing, deploying, and using artificial intelligence systems in an ethical, safe, and trustworthy manner. It aims to align AI technologies with human values and societal expectations while maximizing benefits and minimizing potential risks. Here are some key aspects of responsible AI:

1. Ethical principles: Responsible AI is guided by core ethical principles such as fairness, transparency, privacy, accountability, and safety[1][2]. These principles help ensure AI systems are developed and used in ways that respect human rights and values.

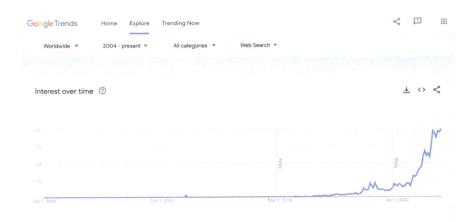

Fig. 3.2 A Google Trends line graph showing the worldwide interest of the term, Responsible AI

2. Fairness and inclusiveness: AI systems should treat all individuals and groups fairly, avoiding bias and discrimination. This involves assessing models for fairness across sensitive attributes like gender, ethnicity, and age[2].

3. Transparency and explainability: AI systems should be designed to be interpretable and explainable, allowing users and stakeholders to understand how decisions are made[1][2].

4. Privacy and security: Strong data governance practices and safeguards should be implemented to protect user privacy and sensitive information[1].

5. Reliability and safety: AI systems must be rigorously tested and monitored to ensure they perform reliably and safely in real-world conditions[2].

6. Accountability: Clear lines of responsibility should be established for the development and deployment of AI systems, with mechanisms for human oversight in critical decision-making processes[1][2].

7. Continuous monitoring and improvement: AI systems should be regularly assessed and updated to address emerging ethical concerns, biases, or issues[1].

8. Interdisciplinary collaboration: Responsible AI development requires input from diverse teams and collaboration with external organizations working on AI ethics[1].

9. Compliance with regulations: AI systems must adhere to relevant laws and regulations governing data protection, fairness, and other ethical considerations[2].

10. Societal impact assessment: The broader implications of AI systems on society should be carefully considered and managed[1].

Implementing responsible AI practices helps build trust in AI technologies, mitigate potential risks, and ensure that AI systems benefit society as a whole. As AI continues to advance rapidly, especially in areas like generative AI, responsible development and deployment become increasingly critical to harness the full potential of these technologies while safeguarding ethical principles and human values[1][2][3].

Citations:

[1] https://www.ibm.com/topics/responsible-ai

[2] https://learn.microsoft.com/en-us/azure/machine-learning/concept-respon sible-ai?view=azureml-api-2

[3] https://www.iso.org/artificial-intelligence/responsible-ai-ethics

[4] https://ai.google/responsibility/responsible-ai-practices/

[5]   https://www.pwc.com/gx/en/issues/artificial-intelligence/what-is-respon sible-ai.html

Compared to their initial versions, these tools have come a long way. As expected, all five AI chatbots give roughly similar responses to the prompt around responsible AI, though Perplexity AI appears to be more comprehensive and behaves more like a search tool than the others. Both Microsoft Copilot and Perplexity cite their sources, and the follow-on prompt by Claude helps to provide examples and useful context.

What these results also demonstrate is the multidimensional nature of what would be considered *Responsible AI*, with trust as an implied foundation. This is something that we must keep in mind regardless of where we are on the AI journey especially for the financial services industry. I do hope that one day, responsible AI would become something so common that we do not need to specifically call out "responsible". But till then, hurdles remain.

Putting Responsible AI in Practice

According to the World Economic Forum, responsible AI is the designing, building, deploying, operationalizing, and monitoring AI systems in a manner that empowers people and businesses and impacts customers and society equitably.[1]

Building with responsible AI principles in mind is crucial not only from a social responsibility perspective, but it also helps to set expectations up front with partners, generates positive stakeholder value, and positions the organization for success. But while establishing guiding principles and boundaries are important, putting it in practice can be challenging.

First and foremost, we need to have common nomenclature, so that different stakeholders from even different jurisdictions can communicate effectively with each other—which will in turn drive adoption of safe, responsible, and trustworthy AI across different parts of the world. While still nascent, the National Institute for Standards and Technology (NIST) in the US is collaborating with the UK Department for Science, Innovation, and Technology (DSIT) and the UK National Physical Laboratory (NPL) to jointly develop a Terminology Tool for Responsible AI, with the goal of facilitating interoperability between UK and US governance frameworks.[2] Looking forward to the future, I do hope that they can expand the scope to incorporate data from other jurisdictions to make it truly global.

In researching for the book, I came across The PRISM Framework, which is used to guide social innovators through the journey of responsible AI implementation for positive social impact.[3] It stresses the importance of organizational readiness over just pure tech capability and highlights the risks and challenges that need to be addressed for an equitable implementation, including data bias.

Briefly speaking, the PRISM Framework builds upon the Presidio Framework by the World Economic Forum (WEF)'s AI Governance Alliance, which funnels a subset of generative AI use cases through three evaluation criteria: business impact, operational readiness, and investment strategy. Meanwhile, the PRISM Framework helps innovators navigate ethical considerations and potential risks when applying AI and offers different adoption pathways and use cases dependent on AI readiness and organization maturity. In considering the ethics capabilities and risks for example, the PRISM Framework highlights four key aspects: Fairness and avoiding bias, ensuring transparency, maintaining accountability, and establishing an ethical AI framework—the blueprint for a responsible AI strategy.

While the PRISM Framework was originally developed for social innovation, how this is used by social innovators for AI can be a model for responsible tech use for a wider adoption as well. After all, transparency, explainability, accountability, and fairness are all essential elements for responsible AI across all sectors. And it is only through collaboration with all stakeholders, including non-profits, governments, universities, and businesses, that we can find pathways to scale AI for social good and harness the technology to the fullest potential to benefit more people.

Spotlight on Nikki Pope, Head of AI & Legal Ethics at NVIDIA
Based on conversation with Nikki Pope. Content has been edited for clarity.

To Nikki, who leads the company's Trustworthy AI initiative, the audience and the context matter when it comes to explainability. Explaining something to a journalist is very different than explaining it to a regulator or a consumer, who you are talking to and what they need to or want to know matter. And we need to consider the differences between industries and regions as well when it comes to what is socially or culturally acceptable. Such nuance is part of the reason why explainability can be inherently difficult.

Consider the now well publicized case where the female partner of Apple co-founder, Steve Wozniak, was offered a lower credit limit for the Apple Card (by Goldman Sachs), calling Goldman Sach's credit decisioning policy into question. Investigations conducted by the New York State Department of Financial Services determined that Goldman Sachs' lending policy and statistical model did not consider prohibited characteristics of the applicants, and the bank did not violate fair lending laws. Rather, difference in credit profiles can lead to different credit offers. For example, if the first applicant has multiple credit cards and a line of credit where the second applicant, in this case, the spouse, only has one credit card, the first applicant's more extensive experience and history of managing credit produce more favorable credit terms than the spouse. So, while on surface, it may appear that Apple Card discriminates against women, the details and transparency matter. And how we offer the explanations to the public versus the regulator also matters.

While it is impossible to build an unbiased machine, there are still ways for us to study how the model will behave and find ways to improve it before it is released. This is where having a diverse community of developers and beta testers can be helpful, as well as mechanisms such as AI model cards, which are used to share essential information about an AI model, including who developed the model and its intended use cases, source and type of training data, performance metrics for different demographics, and mitigation efforts to mitigate unwanted bias, etc. The model cards provide a standardized way to promote transparency and trustworthy AI, both for developer communities and non-technical experts.

But this is also where it can get tricky. "Where bias exists, who ultimately gets to decide what is an acceptable level and what is not?" Nikki asked. There is still work to be done.

In the meantime, we have a lot of opportunity to use AI for good and to find solutions to tough problems that the world is facing now. We can guide toward that future—together.

Whose Responsibility, Is It? We All Have a Role to Play

Eyeing the potential upside of the technology and trying not to be outdone by competitors, organizations around the world have embarked on an AI race. But how do we even begin to set priorities and decide what use cases to pursue with AI or where to invest? Between CFO, CIO, and CTO offices, whose responsibility is it to ensure the technology is deployed responsibly?

While questions such as, "Do we need Chief AI Officer" have started to come up, but what exactly is an AI officer, you may ask?

As the technology continues to evolve, it is becoming even more crucial for everyone to at least gain some level of understanding on how it works—through training and experimentation—to help guide us toward making the right decisions in our day-to-day tasks.

Beyond Chatbots and Image Generators

Between late 2022 to most of 2023, ChatGPT and Dall-E captivated our attention. Things that used to be done by professional artists are now feasible with just a few text prompts.

Unlike previous technology innovation, however, AI doesn't just make things more efficient. It replaces humans in some of the decision-making process. A printing press helped get ideas out faster than writing by hand, but it did not decide what words to print. A car gets us from point A to point B faster than a carriage, but it does not decide on the routes that it will take. An autonomous vehicle on the other hand, *decides* on the route it takes, as well as critical driving decisions such as when the switch lanes, break, or accelerate. The AI that scans through a report and produces a summary *decides* what is important to highlight and to be included in the summary. The algorithm that runs in the background of a search engine *decides* what is important to surface.

And this brings up a very important concept that we will continue to explore throughout the book. Who gets to decide what is included in this new world and how?

There are over 7168 living languages being spoken in the world today. Yet, how many of those are included in the large language models that are being built? With limited high-quality data that can be used for training, what would become of the rich tapestry of our culture? While the problem is not new in the internet world, it will only become exacerbated as the world of living and working becomes more automated and reliant on algorithms, many of which are trained in western languages. The large gap in available data will undoubtedly impact the accuracy of lower resource languages and may even amplify the biases found in their training data, since the text is typically crawled from the open internet.

Not to mention, there are nuances associated with many local languages as well that machines will need to understand. For example, it is customary for native Hongkongers to mix Chinese and English words in the same sentence. As for the Japanese language, three different types of scripts are used, each with its own specific role; and while horizontal text is read left to right, vertical text (like those in novel or manga books) goes from top to bottom with the order of the columns going from right to left.

Ever heard of the saying, lost in translation?

Perhaps it shouldn't come as a surprise when some countries and territories decide to take the driver's seat. Hong Kong, for example, is working on its own local version of the ChatGPT. Interestingly, it is being developed by InnoHK, a government-founded platform, and the government has plans to leverage it internally first before releasing it to the public.[4] Similar approach is being undertaken by other jurisdictions including Brazil and India.

If AI is our new future, what is our role in making sure the diversity of our civilization is not lost, especially for low-resource languages or those where it is simply being spoken but not in written form? Will we be willing to stand up for those who don't have a voice at the table? What part will we play in this new narrative? Or will we simply let it be overwhelmed and washed away, just like the physical islands and coastal nations under threat from climate change?

For AI to act as a tool to help people and nations advance, we must put the tool in the hands of everyone—not just those who can afford it. Who are we designing the solutions for and who are we leaving behind? Does the future of AI lie in fear or hope? Are we shaped by the world we live in, or will we shape it?

In the age of AI abundance, one might argue, the topic of fairness, ethics, and accountability is now more important than ever. But what does this mean in the broader picture?

Key Pillars of Responsible AI

Before we proceed further, it's worth exploring a few real-world examples of the various elements of responsible AI.

Privacy, security, and safety

- Apple's use of differential privacy in iOS to collect user data for improving services while preserving individual privacy.
- The use of human-in-the-loop systems in autonomous vehicles, where human operators can take control if needed.
- The development of AI alignment research programs at organizations like the Future of Humanity Institute and the Center for Human-Compatible AI.

Transparency and explainability

- NVIDIA's Model Card ++ , which provides detailed information about the AI models, including their performance, licensing, limitations, and intended use cases.

Fairness and inclusiveness.

- IBM's AI Fairness 360 toolkit, which helps detect and mitigate unwanted biases in machine learning models.
- Microsoft's groundedness detection API detects whether the large language models (LLMs) product information is reliable and accurate based on what is present in the source materials. The API also provides a correction feature that can automatically change the response to include a corrected text to match the provided grounding source. Such tools can be used as an intermediary to evaluate model outputs and to avoid biased outcomes.

Accountability

- The European Union's AI Act, which would require companies to designate a person responsible for high-risk AI systems.

To put things in a simpler context, I solicited help from a responsible AI expert and practitioner, Noelle Russell, Chief AI Officer from the AI Leadership Institute. Noelle used the analogy of raising baby tigers to explain the evolution of AI models from research to production. When the initial AI models are developed, they are typically purpose built and fun to use. But no one at that moment would be asking the baby tigers questions such as: How big are you going to get? What will you be eating when you grow up? Or what will happen if I don't need you anymore?

To Noelle, these are the essential and important questions that teams need to ask themselves at the very beginning of the development process. The challenge comes when no one really understands that the baby tigers will eventually grow up and cause harm if we are not careful. Who owns the models (the baby tigers in this example), how we train the models (the baby tigers in this example), and what data we are using to train the models matter. We must also carefully consider the consequences—the worst-case scenarios—before the baby tigers grown up.

Credit Decisioning in the Age of AI

The use of AI in credit decisioning provides a good context for Noelle's baby tiger example.

Credit decisioning algorithms play a crucial role in determining access to credit for individuals and businesses. With high volume of data from a wider variety of sources being used in increasingly complex models, financial institutions and fintechs must ensure that proper controls are in place to ensure compliance, privacy, and security, to look for errors and biases in the data that might lead to unintentional consequences, and to ensure adequate protection when it comes to receiving or sharing data with external parties for data modeling.

Credit decisioning algorithms rely on historical data to predict risks and credit worthiness. Unfortunately, bias is ever present in our society and in our data (for example, zip code)—and will persist in algorithms and used in AI systems, leading to potentially disparate outcomes for some demographic groups, especially those from marginalized communities. Even if it is a good intent to have a bias-free system, it is simply unrealistic.

It is worth noting that there are multiple stakeholders in the value chain, including the one that develops the model, the one that secures the data and trains the model, and the one that implements it (e.g. financial institution). As mentioned in the previous chapter, where credit decisions are automated, it is crucial that financial institutions (including fintechs) can explain how the decisions are reached. Such transparency helps consumers and policymakers better understand what drives the outcomes, where improvements can be made, and what best practices need to be established, including for example, privacy by design and human in the loop. The complaints on perceived credit limit discrepancies for Apple Card is a great example. Transparency is also one of the key steps in establishing trust, which is paramount in the financial services industry. Conducting audits and reviews is also a crucial step in ensuring that the decisions are fair and concerns around accountability and liability, especially with third parties, are adequately addressed.

More work is needed to examine different techniques to debias the machine learning models and to create less discriminatory alternative. Further study on fair lending practices is warranted; guidance on issues such as thresholds for disparate outcomes and what constitutes fairness should be established. Close collaboration between fintech startups, incumbent financial institutions, researchers, tech companies, and federal agencies is a must—as it can be a difficult process to thoroughly understand and track how the AI models are trained and deployed.

Care must be taken to ensure that this issue is examined not only from a technical perspective, but also operationally as well, to ensure compliance with Federal law. It is paramount that consumers can maintain trust in the financial services system, and that guardrails are in place to protect their interests and other risks that may arise with the use of AI. Promoting responsible innovation and trustworthiness and preventing discriminatory use of the general-purpose technology must be embedded in the development process from the first day on and through the entire value chain.

Does Accountability Matter?

Over the past few years, AI has evolved in such a lightning speed that at times seems astonishing. But this fast pace demands continuous learning and adaptation. Not only do we need a dynamic operational framework that can adapt as the technology evolves, but we must also acknowledge and address the tension between responsible AI and corporate imperatives, which inevitably could pit ethics against profitability, as evidenced by OpenAI's public turmoil.

A few months after ChatGPT was released in November 2022, I recall being on stage in London talking about the future of AI and addressing the hype around generative AI tools. While it was easy to ride the waves of excitement, I was concerned about the negative consequences the tool has unleashed to the public and the lack of guardrail and questioned if a more responsible path would have been to limit the release. In some ways, I thought it ran counter to the responsible AI path that the non-profit organization was pursuing.

While the fine print was there to inform the public that it was a tool in beta—I thought that the team could have foreseen the potential for abuse. But fine print does little curbing the enthusiasm, so to speak. Tech companies raced to roll out their own flavors of generative AI tools, with the public dazzled by what they thought they could do. The damage is done. The floodgates were opened. And what followed was a somewhat familiar tune of Silicon Valley startup story, and we are left to pick up the pieces.

The turmoil at OpenAI provided a glimpse of the tug of war within the company—the balance between power, purpose, profits, and governance—and Silicon Valley at large. In a dramatic fashion on November 17th, 2023, the non-profit board of OpenAI ousted Sam Altman, the co-founder and CEO of the company, only for him to be reinstated in a matter of few days, after almost all OpenAI employees threatened to quit to work for Microsoft if the board didn't resign.

While we might never know the full extent of the story, which makes an interesting business school case study for years to come, the events that happened leading to and after the saga provided a glimpse of the tug-of-war between those who think AI development needs to accelerate for commercial purposes, and those who want to stay true to the original mission of developing safe AI to benefit all of humanity. Most of the OpenAI board reshuffled after the saga; Ilya Sutskever, OpenAI's chief scientist, one of its co-founders, and one of the old board members, left and founded a new AI company called Safe Superintelligence, aiming to improve AI safety. Co-founder John Schulman left shortly thereafter to join Anthropic. Mira Murati, OpenAI's CTO and one-time interim CEO also announced her departure after 6.5 years with the company, along with research chief Bob McGrew and Barret Zoph. At the time of writing this chapter, OpenAI president and co-founder Greg Brockman had just returned to OpenAI following three months of extended leave, and along with Wojciech Zaremba and Altman were the only co-founders remaining from the original 11-person team.[5] OpenAI has also signaled their intent to convert from a non-profit to for-profit, while pursuing partnerships with consulting companies such as Bain and PricewaterhouseCoopers, to sell AI tools to businesses. The company has one million business customers paying for ChatGPT Enterprise and ChatGPT Edu (ChatGPT for universities) as of October 2024.[6]

Commenting on the board events unfolding, Andrea Bonime-Blanc said it succinctly in her op-ed. "While the innovators are more motivated by riches, influence, and power mostly for themselves and their peers, the governance crowd is more motivated by safety, security, ethics, and guardrails, and thus protecting a broader swath of stakeholders."[7]

In contrast, Apple's approach to artificial intelligence appears more cautious. During its flagship developer conference WWDC24, Apple announced the launch of Apple Intelligence (AI), the company's response to generative AI. The company stressed privacy, safety, and security in their context-aware AI. While many of their AI models will run locally on device the way that the company has long championed, Private Cloud Compute (PCC) will support secure and private AI processing in the cloud for some of the more advanced features that need to be in the cloud.[8]

I do wonder how well Apple Intelligence would perform, especially after witnessing the hallucinations that have plagued the others. Generative AI works by predicting the next word in a sequence to make up a sentence. Since AI doesn't know what's right and what's wrong, it simply chooses its words based on statistics. So dependent on the data that it is being trained on, it could find itself responding to a user's question using what it thought was a relevant (though contextually wrong) answer. In this case, with AI overview telling the user to "eat at least one small rock per day", which was, ironically, based on an article from The Onion.

There are, of course, techniques that can be leveraged to counter the type of hallucinations that we have seen. For example, while generative AI is still used to allow the users to type in questions in a more natural manner, the chatbot will display the results by extracting information directly from a trusted knowledge base, instead of relying on AI, to avoid a wrong answer being randomly generated and presented to the user. This is especially crucial when the users are interfacing with banks or insurance companies, where accuracy and trust are paramount.

For Apple's part, they seemed to be taking notice of some of the concerns that the public has, according to the materials they have released in explaining the foundation models built into Apple Intelligence.[9] Will their data strategy and training help to produce more reliable results? Time will tell. I surely do hope so.

AI as a Mirror of our Reality

AI is largely a mirror reflecting our reality and the data that we feed it. What we use to train the algorithm matters as much as who has access to it. While companies in general have been tight-lipped about their data sources and how their language models are developed, here are a few intriguing points worth noting.

Privacy and Copyrights in the AI-Led World

Can the video that you shared on social media of your one-year kid learning how to walk be used as training data without your consent? What about your monthly op-ed written for an industry publication? Or the eBook that you just published?

Training a large language model such as ChatGPT requires massive amount of useful data. Since inception, OpenAI has signed numerous partnership agreements with publishers, including Time magazine, News Corp, and Financial Times, as well as content sites including Reddit. But not everyone is as enthusiastic as these large publications. According to the Data Provenance Initiative, a collective of independent and academic researchers, web domains are increasingly blocking the crawling of their content to be used to train AI models. While such restrictions are considered essential to protect the interests of the content creators, it will inevitably reduce the amount of available data for training, and the diversity of it.[10]

And even in the world of zettabytes of data, these models will eventually run out of good data for training. What will happen when they grow beyond what can be made available, as some has speculated to happen between 2026 and 2032?[11]

What is fair use and what are our rights when it comes to our digital content being used for training data?

According to the New York Times, OpenAI created Whisper, a speech recognition tool, to transcribe audio from more than one million hours of YouTube videos and podcasts to harvest text to help train its next generation A.I. model GPT-4.[12] While this might seem to be a smart way of getting around the supply problem, the question remains if this may be considered a violation of copyrights of the videos.

The question around copyright will certainly be one that will take a while to play out. At the time of writing this chapter, Meta has paused their plan to train its large language model Meta AI using public Facebook and Instagram posts, images, captions, comments, and stories from users over 18 in the EU due to interjection by the Irish Data Protection Commission (DPC).[13] Shortly after, Brazil's national data protection authority followed suit and blocked Meta from using public posts for AI training, citing the risk of serious and irreparable damage to the fundamental rights of those affected.[14]

This begs the question: Is anything on the open web considered fair use, and can be freely copied and reproduced? How will the content creators be compensated, if at all? And what about content that resides with a news organization or a publisher? Poe, an AI chatbot owned by Quora, already provides users with downloadable HTML files of paywalled articles on demand.[15] And similarly, Perplexity, an AI-powered search service, has been found plagiarizing content crawled from the web.

Part of the complexity of the evolving digital world also stems from the differing approaches that jurisdictions take. In Japan, for instance, AI companies are allowed to learn from images and other materials for commercial purposes, without infringing copyright laws. Its more laissez-faire approach stands in stark contrast to what we see in the EU—and such patchwork approach could hinder innovation as tech companies will need to navigate around country- or region-specific rules, as we have witnessed.

But beyond copyrights, there are other concerns as well. What about videos that are created by children or featuring children? What are their rights and how can they be protected? LAION-5B, an AI dataset that has been built from Common Crawl snapshots of the internet, was found by Human Rights Watch (HRW) to contain images of real children from Brazil and Australia. According to the HRW report, identifiable information such as full name, ages, and name of preschool could be found in the link to one of the photos.[16] In another, the YouTube video was marked as unlisted and otherwise undiscoverable in searches. As with anything else on the Internet, once a digital copy is out there, it can be referenced and used in datasets to train AI. And once it has been used, it cannot really be "forgotten".

In some situations, this creates cultural concerns and harm beyond the *obvious* as well. For example, reproduction of photos of deceased people during periods of mourning is forbidden for First Nations peoples. And it is impossible to control when their images are reproduced if they are included in the AI training.

To combat the growing impact of AI-generated content on its platform, YouTube has quietly updated its privacy guidelines to allow people to request the removal of synthetic content that resembles their face or voice, using YouTube's privacy complaint process. Removal is not guaranteed, and it remains to be seen if this would indeed be useful in deterring privacy violations and protecting the rights of individuals.

As is typical in a fast-evolving space, there are more questions that have yet to be unanswered. Balancing risks and benefits, and protecting the privacy and rights of the public, especially those who are the most vulnerable, must be top priority when it comes to innovation. It is a journey that we need to undertake and explore together. The only way that we can harness the transformative power of AI for good and ensure that it can be leveraged by many is through collaboration and intention to do what is right.

The Authentic Voice

Around the topic of transparency and cultivating trust, authenticity matters. What happens when your voice can be altered with a click of a button?

Softbank is developing an AI-powered capability called SoftVoice, for call center representatives to soften the voice if the tool detects yelling or an angry tone.[17] While this might be deemed helpful for call center reps who are at the receiving end of an agitated incoming call so that they wouldn't be subjected to an angry voice, should the callers be notified that their voice has been altered? And if the technology is available for operators to change the tone of the voice, what comes next? Will the words in the conversation be altered as well?

Consider another use case. What if the voice is not digitally altered; rather it is being generated by a program out of necessity and with your consent? Much has been written and discussed on the potential pitfalls of voice cloning, especially in the hands of bad actors. But for those with medical conditions who have lost their voice, the ability to recreate it through artificial intelligence can be a life changing experience. For example, US representative Jennifer Wexton (D-Va.) was diagnosed with Parkinson's-like condition known as progressive supranuclear palsy (PSP), which severely impacted her ability to communicate verbally. Using audio clips of Wexton before the onset of the neurological disorder, ElevenLabs was able to clone her voice and her tone.[18]

The congresswoman's story highlights the duality of AI that this book aims to highlight: While the technology has tremendous power to improve the well-being of many in the society, it can also bring about extraordinary threats when used with the wrong intention in the hands of bad actors. Context and responsibilities matter.

To some, this may seem to be slippery slope in the making. For others, this gives them a second chance that they otherwise wouldn't have. To ensure that we can continue to innovate in a responsible manner, however, it is more urgent than ever to have the proper guardrails in place—and ensure balance and transparency as the technology develops.

Third Party Risks

Ensuring humans remain at every step in the development and execution of AI is one way of maintaining balance and transparency as the technology continues to evolve. This is crucial not only from a legal and governance perspective, but also from a reputational exposure one.

As we become more dependent on third-party providers, we must ensure that these providers can demonstrate that their systems function as intended, that they are transparent with the data they use to train the models, and that they have taken the necessary steps to detect and reduce bias.

One example is the use of surveillance pricing products in financial services, where advanced algorithms and artificial intelligence are used in combination of historical and real-time customer data, including location, credit history, and purchase behavior. Often, such technology is developed and offered by a third party outside of the financial institution, creating a layer of opacity in an ecosystem of intermediaries that can impact the end consumers.

A Fairer Data Economy

Is a fairer data economy possible? Or is it a fallacy? In the absence of regulation, will self-regulation hold water?

The discussion around the value and control of data has gained increasing prominence with advances in web3. And it remains to be seen if, and when, we can get to a future where we can retain more control over our own data, and where the benefits will accrue to individuals and our communities.

In the race toward dominance, where billions of venture funding is at stake, it would at times appear that delivering commercial value for shareholders must take precedence over anything else. But such win-at-all-costs attitudes assume that social responsibility bears no substantial value—a topic that we will explore further in Chapter 8.

If AI were to play a dominant role in our collective future, and I believe it will, then it is even more urgent than ever that we instill fairness and responsible development principles as part of our DNA. With technology as powerful as what we have to-date, we simply cannot afford to unleash it without guardrails and controls in place. We have seen that movie many times over and we know how it ends.

While AI may reflect or even amplify fragments of the world that we live, it also has the power to influence and create a new reality that we will find ourselves in. What kind of future do we want to be in? And what is the legacy that we want to leave our children and the generations after them? Technology progress should not and must not come at the expense of those who are marginalized and lack the power to dictate this future that they are very much a part of.

Going back to our original question: Can we truly use AI for good? How can we best leverage the power of community to create the future that we want for ourselves, the next generations, and thereafter?

In the next section, we will deep dive in the world of AI in financial services, and the risks and opportunities of our new AI-led reality.

Notes

1. Responsible AI Playbook for Investors, World Economic Forum, June 2024. https://www3.weforum.org/docs/WEF_Responsible_AI_Playbook_for_Investors_2024.pdf
2. Assuring a responsible future for AI, Gov.UK, 6 November, 2024. https://www.gov.uk/government/publications/assuring-a-responsible-future-for-ai
3. AI for Impact: The PRISM Framework for Responsible AI in Social Innovation, World Economic Forum, June 2024. https://www3.weforum.org/docs/WEF_AI_for_Impact_Prism_Framework_2024.pdf
4. Entire govt to use city's own ChatGPT this year, rthk.hk, 13 July 2024, https://news.rthk.hk/rthk/en/component/k2/1761421-20240713.htm
5. H Field, OpenAI co-founder Greg Brockman returns after three months of leave, CNBC, 12 November 2024. https://www.cnbc.com/2024/11/12/openai-co-founder-greg-brockman-returns-after-three-months-of-leave.html

6. B Lin, OpenAI, Bain Expand AI Partnership to Sell ChatGPT to Businesses, The Wall Street Journal, 17 October 2024. https://www.wsj.com/articles/openai-bain-expand-ai-partnership-to-sell-chatgpt-to-businesses-d17775dc

7. A Bonime-Blanc, The OpenAI Governance Crisis: Early Tech Company Lessons, National Association of Corporate Directors, 25 Jan 2024. https://www.nacdonline.org/all-governance/governance-resources/directorship-magazine/online-exclusives/2024/January2024/OpenAI-governance-crisis-early-tech-company-lessons/

8. Private Cloud Compute: A new frontier for AI privacy in the cloud, Apple, 10 June 2024. https://security.apple.com/blog/private-cloud-compute/

9. Introducing Apple's On-Device and Server Foundation Models, Apple, 10 June 2024. https://machinelearning.apple.com/research/introducing-apple-foundation-models

10. Consent in crisis: The rapid decline of the AI data commons. https://www.dataprovenance.org/Consent_in_Crisis.pdf

11. A Tremayne-Pengelly, A.I. Companies Are Running Out of Training Data: Study, Observer, 19 July 2024. https://observer.com/2024/07/ai-training-data-crisis/

12. C Metz, How Tech Giants Cut Corners to Harvest Data for A.I., New York Times, 6 April 2024. https://www.nytimes.com/2024/04/06/technology/tech-giants-harvest-data-artificial-intelligence.html

13. A Belanger, Meta halts plans to train AI on Facebook, Instagram posts in EU, Ars Technica, 14 June 2024. https://arstechnica.com/tech-policy/2024/06/meta-halts-plans-to-train-ai-on-facebook-instagram-posts-in-eu/

14. Euronews with AP, Brazilian regulator bans Meta from using data for AI training, Euro News, 4 July 2024. https://www.euronews.com/next/2024/07/04/brazilian-regulator-bans-meta-from-using-data-for-ai-training

15. T Marchman, Quora's Chatbot Platform Poe Allows Users to Download Paywalled Articles on Demand, Wired, 28 July 2024. https://www.wired.com/story/quora-chatbot-poe-download-paywalled-articles/

16. A Belanger, AI trains on kids' photos even when parents use strict privacy settings, Ars Technica, 2 July 2024. https://arstechnica.com/tech-policy/2024/07/ai-trains-on-kids-photos-even-when-parents-use-strict-privacy-settings/

17. K Irwin, This 'Emotion-Canceling' AI Alters Angry Voices for Call Center Staff, PCMag, 19 June 2024, https://www.pcmag.com/news/softbank-emotion-canceling-ai-alters-angry-voices-for-call-center-staff
18. G Schneider, Rep. Wexton, confronting degenerative disease, finds her voice through AI, Washington Post, 13 July 2024. https://www.washingtonpost.com/dc-md-va/2024/07/13/virginia-wexton-congress-ai-voice/

4

Size Matters When Adopting and Scaling AI

Behind the glitzy generative front lies the extractive dark side of the technology.

In one of the talks that I delivered to a group of talented young adults in 2024, someone in the audience asked: "How important are people when it comes to startup innovation?".

As I often stress, our work is always about serving the community and elevating the vibrancy of the cultures that are embedded within our ecosystems. Just as the logo of our company—a dandelion seed—symbolizing the propagation of ideas and opportunities in different corners, regardless of demographics.

And therein lies one of the most important lessons of our times: technology is merely a means to an end. It should be anyway. It can be used to break down the physical barriers that separate us and facilitate exchange of ideas, but it also be used to create roadblocks between economies and cultures. It can create a pathway for more people to turn their dreams and aspirations to reality, but it can also exacerbate the divide between the haves and have-nots.

Technology can bring us closer to one another or push us further apart. Where will the realities of AI bring us depends not only on what the technology can do, but who has the power to influence who the technology serves and for what purpose.

What we do today will influence which version of the future prevails. The irony is the society's greatest challenges transcend corporate walls and national boundaries. Collaboration, not division, is the only viable way forward.

T. Lau, *Banking on (Artificial) Intelligence*, https://doi.org/10.1007/978-3-031-81647-5_4

As the Italian proverb goes: *Se Atene piange Sparta non ride*. We are all in the same boat.

In this chapter, we will look at who are the big tech players in AI and how they are shaping the industry. We will also discuss AI adoption readiness in financial services and the top players in innovation and talent acquisition.

What are the biggest obstacles to achieving "greatness"? What have we learned in the past in the evolution of the internet and technology adoption that can be applied now? Can monopolies be prevented (Fig. 4.1)?

Fig. 4.1 Size matters when adopting and scaling AI

An Expensive Endeavor

Unfortunately, training and re-training models doesn't come *cheap*. In this case, scale matters. To realize AI's true potential, companies need access to capabilities that lie with a limited pool of human experts, along with capital to support expensive and resource-intensive infrastructure. This sticker shock will likely further benefit the few big corporations and countries with deep pockets—effectively monopolizing an industry that could otherwise have helped lessen inequality in our society instead of deepening it.

So how much does it cost to train an AI model? While it is not an exact science and hardware and energy costs, training duration, and staff expenses can vary quite significantly, the report by Epoch AI shed some light on the subject. According to their study, which was also cited in the AI Index Report published by the Stanford University, the cloud compute cost to train OpenAI's GPT-4 was estimated to be around $78 million; and for Google's Gemini 1.0 Ultra, it was about $191 million.[1] At the current rate, it is estimated that training for the largest model may cost more than a billion dollars by 2027.

Which begs the obvious question. Who can afford it?

The Incumbent and the Startups

Truth is, we might already know the answer. As the saying goes, history does not repeat itself, but it often rhymes. Wealth begets wealth; size (and scale) matters. As it turns out, something similar can be said about AI. We can look at the journey of a powerhouse AI startup Inflection AI and its co-founder, Mustafa Suleyman, for instance.

Mustafa Suleyman co-founded DeepMind in London in 2010, which Google acquired in January 2014 for £400 m, one of the largest European acquisitions made by Google at the time. As we saw in Chapter 1, DeepMind's AlphaGo stunned the world and defeated Go champion Lee Sedol in 2016. Suleyman eventually left DeepMind in 2019 and joined the parent company Google until 2022, to become venture capitalist at Greylock Partners.[2]

Shortly thereafter, Suleyman co-founded Inflection AI, an AI studio with Reid Hoffman and Karén Simonyan, and raised $225 million in a first round of funding from Greylock, Microsoft, Reid Hoffman, Bill Gates, Eric Schmidt, Mike Schroepfer, Demis Hassabis, Will.i.am, Horizons Ventures, and Dragoneer. All in, Inflection AI brought in over $1.5 billion, with NVIDIA being included in the last round of funding in June 2023.

In March 2024, Microsoft hired Mustafa Suleyman and Karén Simonyan to form a new Microsoft AI group, focusing on advancing Microsoft's Copilot and other consumer AI products. Additional members from Inflection AI, including AI engineers and researchers, also joined the team at Microsoft, which bought nonexclusive rights to sell access to the Inflection AI model through Azure Cloud. The startup also announced plans to expand Pi, a popular personal AI assistant like ChatGPT, into the enterprise.

It is unclear what would happen to Inflection AI in the long run. While it is not an acquisition per se, it feels like one, especially when your leadership teams and tech talent are recruited away.

Could this be the beginning of a trend? In June 2024, Adept, an AI startup with the goal to develop AI agents, announced that their co-founders and some of Adept's employees would be joining Amazon AGI team (artificial general intelligence), and the e-commerce giant would be licensing Adept's agent technology.[3] Similarly, Amazon pursued a non-exclusive license to the robotic foundation models of Covariant, a Bay Area-based startup that builds advanced AI models to enable robots to see and act on the world around them; included in the deal was the hiring of the company's co-founders and a quarter of their employees.[4]

Character.AI announced a similar deal with Google; the startup would grant Google a fee in the amount of $2.7 billion to license their LLM technology, and their co-founders, who were also former Googlers, would leave the startup and return to Google.[5] The interesting thing to note is that the deal was forged because Google wanted Noam Shazeer, Character.AI's founder, to return to Google and help build Gemini.

Inflection AI, Adept, Character.AI, and Covariant represent a cautionary tale for other AI startups in the ecosystem that are building their own large language models. In this business, it is hard to compete with the big tech giants with deep pockets; developing cutting-edge technology before a steady and robust revenue stream is established can be hard to sustain. It remains to be seen, however, how long the regulators would allow similar deals going forward, especially given potential antitrust concerns.

Will AI be a Divider or an Equalizer?

When the internet was born, it was envisioned that it would serve as an equalizer between those who have access to resources, and those who don't. Never has information flown so freely and quickly, transcending physical boundaries of countries and time zones. The world is your oyster, as the saying goes. And everything is open, if you are willing to take the opportunity to learn.

But as the world becomes more digital, companies soon realize the tremendous power that they hold with our data. Not only with the ability to monetize it, but also to gain insights into our everyday lives and shape our social circles and our actions.

Technology innovation is not just about what the invention itself can bring; it is also about power and positioning, with companies and economies pitting against each other. On a micro level, it is competition for dominance between Silicon Valley versus New York City and Boston. On a macro level, it is the East versus the West, and increasingly, the Middle East. Against the backdrop of protectionism and rising nationalism, tensions between nations and regions help shape the trajectory of mega companies and the regulations that govern them.

As AI plays an increasingly prominent role in our lives, is history doomed to repeat itself? Will the world be further divided into the haves and have-nots? And what happens when an AI arms race becomes a self-fulfilling prophecy with each party trying to assert dominance? Where will escalating competition—instead of collaboration—lead us?

AI Safety

While there may not be a doomsday clock for AI, the topic of AI safety is relevant here.

Much has been said about OpenAI and their decision to release ChatGPT while the tool was in beta. But I'd suspect not everyone is aware of the opposite decision that their rival, Anthropic, made a few months prior. Anthropic, a US-based AI research company and a public benefit corporation, was founded by former members of OpenAI, Daniela Amodei, and Dario Amodein in early 2021. The latter joined OpenAI in 2016 and left in 2021 while he was VP of research.

According to an interview with TIME magazine, Dario Amodei indicated in the summer of 2022, a few months before OpenAI launched ChatGPT, he was faced with a similar decision with their AI chatbot, Claude.[6] Ultimately, they decided to withhold the launch to allow more time to conduct internal safety testing. Amodei indicated that his decision was driven primarily by the worry around the potential consequences of releasing such a powerful tool, and that he wanted to avoid triggering a race to build something potentially even more powerful and dangerous.

Unfortunately, as we have since learned, Sam Altman, CEO of OpenAI, a rival company, unleashed ChatGPT into the world soon after. And just as Amodei had predicted, this action triggered an AI arms race and a frenzy of AI hype and capital injection, not just between companies but amongst countries.

In August 2024, the US Artificial Intelligence Safety Institute, housed within NIST, announced agreements with OpenAI and Anthropic to enable US AI Safety Institute to review and test their major new models prior to and following their public release, with the goal of evaluating capabilities and safety risks, and methods to mitigate them.[7]

However, it is worthwhile to note that such collaborations, as well as Anthropic's Responsible Scaling Policy—a commitment to not release AI above a certain level until certain safety guardrails are in place—are entirely voluntary. The Biden administration's executive order on AI, where the US AI Safety Institute at NIST was created, is not legislation, and can be overturned by the next president.

This is, nevertheless, a good step in the right direction. Time will tell if this holds true in the long run, especially when capital requirements increase and create a potential conflict between profits and good intention. Personally, I believe that the most reliable way to ensure safe and responsible development requires proper regulatory framework to be in place, instead of relying on the goodwill of a private company CEO.

In Chapter 9, we will dig deeper into the state of regulations on AI around the world, from the first international treaty on the use of AI and the EU Artificial Intelligence Act, to the White House Executive Order and upcoming UK AI Bill.

The Talent Grab

Fulfilling the AI ambition requires talent. Unfortunately, while the opportunity is vast and the demand is strong, the talent pool remains somewhat limited. Between the private sectors, the public institutions, and academia, those with scale and resources are often the ones with the most advantage in attracting the retaining the right talent.

According to the 2024 Evident AI Index, JP Morgan Chase tops the index for the third year in a row, and it is the only financial institution ranked the top 3 across all four pillars of the index: talent, innovation, leadership, and transparency. The share of AI talent in the bank represents 8.5% of all AI talent across the 50 Index banks, and it expanded their talent pool at 16.1%, the largest year-over-year in the industry.[8] Unsurprisingly, JP Morgan Chase leads in AI research, representing 35% of all AI researchers affiliated with the banks included in the index.

All said, of the top 10 banks in the overall Index, five of them are US banks: JP Morgan Chase, Capital One, Wells Fargo, Citigroup, and Morgan Stanley. These five banks also account for 42% of AI talent across the Index banks, with an astonishing 39% year-over-year growth.

The dominance of US banks also echoes the lead that US has when it comes to venture funding on AI startups and the vibrancy of the American AI ecosystem. The lead in AI talent capability and AI development capability by the US banks indicates that the dominance will likely continue into the foreseeable future. And this extends beyond banking as well. The UK government's Institute for AI Safety, for instance, announced their first AI Safety Institute overseas office in San Francisco in May 2024, which enables the office to tap into the tech talent pool in the Bay Area and engage with the innovation teams based in the area.[9]

While the US produces some of the largest and most well-known AI startups, and the larger banks and big tech companies are well-positioned due to their access to capital and data, the regional hubs in Europe with their lineup of scale-ups and educational institutions are equally vibrant as well. After all, DeepMind was founded in London in 2010, before it was acquired by Google in 2014 and merged with Google Brain division in Google AI. UK is home to some of the best educational institutions for AI, including University of Oxford, Imperial College London, University College London, and University of Cambridge. It should therefore not be surprising that the country is one of the AI startup hotspots outside of the US and China, along with Israel, Germany, and France.

It suffices to say that the competition for talent is also not limited to the American soil only. In France, for example, where famed computer scientist Yann LeCun is from, French AI startups including Mistral AI, Poolside (a newly minted unicorn in June 2024), and H (previously known as Holistic AI), are all vying for the same talent as big tech companies.

Despite the broader economic uncertainty, consolidations, and persistent cost cutting and staff redundancy programs, the AI sector overall continues to grow. The total number of AI job postings increased over 14% quarter-on-quarter (QoQ) in Q1 2024, and AI job listings accounted for over 11% of all job listings posted over the past year. Unsurprisingly, the demand for expertise greatly outpaces supply, and it is beginning to have a dampening effect on AI adoption and preventing financial institutions from being able to fully benefit from the technology. In a study conducted by Mastercard and Fintech Nexus, half of the respondents cited a shortage of data science resources and modeling capacity to be a barrier to widely adopting AI for detecting fraud and money laundering.[10]

This begs the question. As academia, big tech companies, startups, and financial institutions are all competing for the same talent, who will get their pick? Who stands to benefit and who will lose out in the talent war?

If the insights from the Stanford AI Index are of any indication, academia has been suffering from a brain drain of AI experts to the private sector, with a growing share of PhDs pursuing careers in the industry. According to the report, while the percentage of new AI PhD graduates who joined academia was roughly the same as those who joined the industry in 2011, the figures began to diverge greatly. By 2022, roughly 70.7% chose to work in the industry after graduating, versus 19.95% in academia. Meanwhile, the figures heading for government work remained around 0.76%.[11]

AI Economy: A Global Agenda

The private and public sectors have always intertwined. Leveraging government funding and policy to finance cutting edge research and development, and to boost a country's competitiveness and growth in targeted sectors isn't new. After all, government grants and federal contracts played a significant role in transforming Silicon Valley into the global powerhouse of technology innovation that it is today, and the Advanced Technology Vehicle Manufacturing loan program provided funding to Telsa at a critical juncture in 2010. Likewise, the CHIPS and Science Act of 2022 promise to strengthen America's semiconductor industry, a crucial component for the digital economy, as well as for future growth and innovation.

Beyond the US, other regions are also gearing up for the future AI economy, albeit at various speed and levels of urgency. As we embark on a discovery journey, it is crucial for us to approach it with an open mindset. AI as a technology is multifaceted; its opportunities are immense, and impact is profound. The challenges that we face in our society affect all of us and are not bound by physical borders; only through collaboration so that we can harness the transformative power of AI ethically and responsibly—together.

The inception of an international network for AI safety by different countries including US, UK, Canada, Japan, South Korea, and Singapore gives me hope for an open dialogue toward a safe and ethical AI future.

Here are a few examples on the AI agenda pursued by various jurisdictions. This list is by no means exhaustive.

Australia

Australia first published their AI Action Plan in 2021 as part of the Australian Government's Digital Economy Strategy, to help deliver a modern and leading digital economy by 2030, with an emphasis on becoming a global leader in trusted, secure, and responsible AI.

Much of the plan involves new investments of $124.1 million in building out the country's AI capability, backed by government grants for the development and adoption of new AI solutions for regional and national challenges, as well as talent development.[12] It also includes the creation of National Artificial Intelligence Centre (NAIC) to support AI adoption for SMEs, to foster the creation of an AI ecosystem in Australia,[13] and to uplift safe and responsible AI practice—a focal point that we will review more in Chapter 10.

Of note, however, $11 million funding originally allocated in the AI Action Plan to establish four new Artificial Intelligence and Digital Capability Centres has been repurposed as of August 2024.[14] Nevertheless, the government has moved forward with several initiatives aimed at promoting responsible AI development. We will look at them in further detail later in the book.

Brazil

Brazil's government unveiled a R$ 23 billion (a little over US $4 billion) proposal for an AI investment plan that is aimed at reducing tech dependency on international technology giants.[15] The initiative also includes specific goals such as developing Portuguese-language AI models reflecting Brazil's cultural and linguistic heritage.

The investment in AI reflects a global trend observed elsewhere, including the US, UK, Canada, China, India, and Israel. The focus on developing their own AI models based on the Portuguese language is also understandable but significant. After all, as mentioned earlier in the book, much of the models have been developed by American big tech companies and in English.

This raises an important question, again: What happens to the other countries who can't afford to develop their own models based on their own language and cultures? Either due to the monetary resources required—or simply—not enough data that can be used for training?

China

Compared to other jurisdictions, China is closely matched with the US in terms of the level of dedication and ambition toward AI development, which dates to 2015 when macro-level AI policies first emerged, and the introduction of the 13th Five-Year-Plan for National Economic and Social Development of the People Republic of China. More policy papers soon followed.

According to the latest plan, China aims to become the world's major AI innovation center by 2030.[16] To get there, the country has focused on developing AI talent pipeline and introduced new policies to promote innovation efforts and application development around the country. It ranks second globally in terms of number of newly funded AI startups between 2013 and 2023, behind the US but ahead of the UK, Israel, Canada, and France. The country also led the world with the most industrial robotics installed, accounting for more than half of the global total according to Stanford University's AI Index Report 2024.[17] As an aging nation with 21 percent of its population being over 60 years old, automation (using robotics) serves as a key avenue to help improve productivity.

Saudi Arabia

Similar to the other nations in the Middle East, Saudi Arabia's AI ambitions are vast. Led by the Saudi Data & AI Authority (SDAIA), the Kingdom's overall AI strategy seeks to position Saudi Arabia as a global leader amongst data-driven economies by 2030, with an infusion of $100 billion for technology, out of which $40 billion is earmarked just for AI.[18] As recent as November 2024, there are also reports of another new state-backed AI project called Project Transcendence, that will focus on recruiting new talent and develop the local ecosystem.[19]

The massive efforts point to Saudia Arabia's desire to become a global data and AI hub—powered by a large local and international network of partners, supportive policies and regulatory environment, investments in best-in-class research environment and economic development, as well as training programs to foster AI and technology skills development for the Kingdom's young population.

The Vision 2030 strategy lays out a phase-approach and ambitious metrics, with the first phase focusing on building out the national talent and local ecosystem, as well as setting up the regulatory environment and investment vehicles. Whereas phase two will focus on global. Some of the key metrics include having 40% of their workforce trained on basic data and AI literacy skills and developing more than 300 active startups in the data and AI sector. Priority sectors include education, healthcare, energy, smart city, and government.

United Arab Emirates

Omar Sultan Al Olama was appointed the Minister of State for Artificial Intelligence for the United Arab Emirates—the first such position in the world.[20] It reflects the UAE's ambition to become one of the world's leading nations in AI by 2031, and ultimately the best country in the world by 2071, in alignment with UAE Centennial 2071.[21] The kingdom believes that its AI Strategy will contribute positively to education, economy, government development, as well as community happiness. A series of policy papers followed,

The priority sectors, as outlined in the AI strategy document, include resources & energy, logistics & transport, tourism & hospitality, healthcare, and cybersecurity. These priorities are chosen based on the potential economic gains from AI deployment, with the opportunity estimated to be at AED 335 billion (over US $90 billion), an equivalent to 26% increase.[22]

Developing an ecosystem requires funding, talent, and regulatory support. With majority of AI startups currently being in the US, UK, and China, along with emphasis on AI research and development in these regions, the UAE will need to provide significant incentives to compete for the same pool of foreign investment and talent. Raising awareness for UAE citizens, upskilling/reskilling professionals, and training the next generation to develop a local talent pipeline will be critical as well. This holds true for all the regions aspiring to be part of the future AI-led economy.

United Kingdom

Like all the other countries, the UK seeks a national strategy to capture the benefits of the AI economy. Launched in 2021, the National AI Strategy for the UK lays out a 10-year plan to invest and plan for the long-term needs of the UK AI ecosystem, to encourage research and development, innovation, investment, and talent development, while protecting the public's interests and ensuring the technology benefits all sectors and regions.[23]

It's worth noting that while AI presents a series of challenges and opportunities for different countries, many of the themes are not new to the UK due to the country's long history with the technology. According to the 2024 AI Index Report published by the Stanford Institute for Human-Centered Artificial Intelligence, the UK ranked third in originating the number of foundation models released since 2019, as well as the amount of private investment in AI, behind the US and China.[24] The country also had the highest number of AI university study program in English, ahead of the US and Canada.

There is work to be done, however, especially around job opportunities and AI talent. For example, according to the same report, the number of AI job postings lacks behind that of US, Canada, and Australia, as well as other European countries including Spain, Sweden, Belgium, Netherlands, France, Switzerland, and Austria. And the net AI talent migration also lacks that of other European countries such as Luxembourg, Switzerland, Cyprus, and Germany.

To ensure that the country continues to remain in the forefront of the AI innovation ecosystem, the UK National AI Strategy specifically calls out the need to attract and train a diverse range of talent and skillsets to help develop and deliver the innovation needed, along with the need for a pro-innovation business environment and capital market.

In October 2024, the FCA launched an AI Lab to help the financial services industry address challenges as it relates to responsible development of AI technologies.[25] It includes four key components: AI Spotlight, AI Sprint, AI Input Zone, and Supercharged Sandbox, with the goal of promoting dialogs and collaboration between the financial services industry, tech industry, academia, and regulatory bodies.

From Concept to Production

While it is pretty evident that the technology is having an impact on how we live and how we work, and as fascinating as some of the statistics may appear, there are still so many unknowns when it comes to exactly *how* the technology will impact economies and industries.

For example, how much will the increase in interest in AI translate to actual proof of concept (POC) projects? How many POCs will turn into long-term deployment and in what areas? And how much return-on-investment (ROI) will the deployment lead to?

Spotlight on SAVVI AI
Based on conversation with Maya Mikhailov, Founder & CEO of SAVVI AI.

When embarking on an AI journey, organizations should first ask themselves: "Do we have a problem or opportunity that is operationally relevant, backed by data we have collected, occurs with enough frequency, and aligns with our strategic priorities?" These questions help pinpoint where AI can drive real value and ROI. Next, consider talent and resources. Not every organization wants or needs an AI Center of Excellence with data scientists, engineers, and dedicated AI infrastructure. Many prefer to leverage AI outcomes without building everything from scratch. This is when you assess your internal talent—identifying budding data leaders—and decide whether to partner with external partners or use existing teams and tools to meet AI goals. Finally, organizations need to focus on change management. Often, the technology itself isn't the biggest challenge; it's ensuring that employees aren't threatened by AI and the process changes it brings. Bringing stakeholders into the conversation early and educating them on how AI complements, not replaces, their roles will ease adoption and help AI be seen as a tool for success rather than a competitive coworker looking to take their job.

It is a common misconception that it is difficult-to-nearly-impossible to incorporate AI into legacy systems. However, even the most antiquated infrastructure often produces forms of tabular data, like that weekly Excel spreadsheet in your inbox. This tabular data can be used to feed an AI system to find insights and optimizations. Not all AI requires "vectorized streaming data systems" to achieve any business results. One of the biggest mistakes I see in legacy organizations that are considering AI is summed up as "prerequisite paralysis." These organizations believe they must completely rebuild their core data processes and infrastructure before they can even start addressing even the most basic AI use cases. This leads to long, costly overhauls—with timelines of 24 months or more on just the re-architecture. Inevitably, the CFO or board asks, "What have we achieved so far for this spend?" The answer, "We're setting up to start our AI journey in two years," doesn't cut it. Especially not when nimble competitors pull farther away.

The cleverest companies are iterating with what they already have, proving value with shorter-term wins, and using those results to justify future investments in updated infrastructure. This approach allows them to build momentum for AI and systems updates while mapping out a scalable AI strategy over time.

In today's market, AI solutions exist for both small and large financial institutions. Smaller institutions can leverage external partners and tools, offering them flexibility and speed, while larger ones may build in-house teams and infrastructure to capitalize on AI at scale fully. While "legacy" often suggests an inability to innovate, let alone catch up with the market, success with AI comes down to an institution's attitude toward data, not its age.

Does the financial institution see data as a competitive advantage to improve efficiency, reduce risk, and fuel growth, or merely as a byproduct of operations and a burden of a regulated industry? Those that treat data as an untapped asset, ready to unlock a wealth of answers and improve decisioning, regardless of their legacy systems, will find paths to AI that match their size, resources, and goals.

Ultimately, a commitment to unlocking value from data, not size or legacy alone, determines AI readiness.

What Does an AI-Ready Bank Look Like?

With interest and innovation ramping up, how prepared are banks to adopt and respond to rapidly evolving technology?

Having secured the talent is only one part of the equation. To move beyond consumers of technology to become drivers of innovation, financial institutions need to be able to leverage the talent to further develop intellectual property and deploy the technology to address the needs of the bank. They also need to have the right tech stack and data strategy in place to take advantage of the technology, as well as the right culture to create the change needed. As tempting as it might be to think of AI as an isolated capability that can be added on, it is not something that can be created in vacuum. While data is the fuel that powers the AI models and enables financial institutions to create personalized experiences for their customers, and there is such an abundance of data available, getting to the state where it can be used is easier said than done. I will explain why.

Almost three decades ago when I relocated to the New York, I opened a bank account with a large global financial institution. After I moved to Washington D.C., I opened another bank account locally—as was customary at the time. Through the years, as the bank transforms, these two accounts remain separate: two ATM cards, two online banking logins, and two statements. When I created my small business over 7 years ago, I thought the best way to manage the finance would be to have everything under one bank: So I opened a small business account with the same bank. But instead of making things simpler as I thought it would be, now I must juggle between three ATM cards, three online banking logins, and three sets of statements.

To make things even more interesting, although the bank has been billing me for services for the past few decades, the teller at the bank branch was not able to locate the record digitally when I visited the branch. It was then I realized that the bank branch has been keeping a handwritten record of my safety deposit box in a tin box. So much for digital transformation? The irony.

Imagine the rich insights the bank would have gotten on me as a customer of over 30 years, if it had managed to bring the data together and connect the dots along the various customer journeys with me as a consumer and a small business owner. Instead, the data remains siloed across different departments, leaving behind golden opportunities to create more value for customers and better anticipate or meet their needs, beyond traditional transactions.

Of course, developing the infrastructure to collect and analyze the data is just the first step. Figuring out what data is needed and how the data can be used—including developing or investing in the tools needed to harness the insights is the critical next step, in preparation for the journey forward with the technology partner and build a true data-driven organization.

We will continue the focus on AI-ready bank in the next chapter from the perspective of trust and risk management.

Spotlight on Raiffeisen Bank International AG

Based on conversation with Vanja Tokic from Raiffeisen Bank International AG, one of the leading banking groups in Austria and Central and Eastern Europe.

Digital transformation is not a "one and done" exercise. We need to go through multiple iterations, learn from our mistakes, and continue to improve over a long period of time. We also need to shift our thinking and ask: "What can we improve on from where we are now?".

In every transformation project in banking, there are two crucial areas that we must address: core banking systems and data. "What do we do with the decades-old core banking system?" is a familiar question that many banks face.

Should we work around what we have because it's too complex and expensive to modernize, or do we build a new stack from scratch?

Similar challenges exist with data. To create a digital and AI-enabled future of banking, you need to first get your data in order—encompassing data governance, cleansing, processing, and management. This is foundational, but unfortunately, it is not a sexy topic that many are eager to discuss. Nevertheless, there is significant work to be done, and we can already use large-language AI models and agents to assist data analysts and engineers in finding, sorting, cleaning, and organizing data.

The tech debt of legacy financial institutions creates an opportunity for newer banks in emerging economies to develop new capabilities in a more agile manner. Incumbents will eventually need to play catch up, not just from a system development and process perspective, but also from a cultural and mindset perspective. This is another area where we can leverage AI to perform code conversion and update the legacy systems in a more efficient manner.

When it comes to the hot topic of customer-facing AI, how to deploy generative AI for external facing applications in a safe manner is top of mind for many organizations. As trust is at the core of our banking system, ensuring accurate responses and minimizing the potential for AI hallucinations is crucial. Here, Vanja offers this advice: keep humans in the loop. Use generative AI to generate questions and answers, validate the results, finetune, repeat, and refine. And for some particularly sensitive topics, we may want to be more prescriptive with the answers.

But we are merely scratching the surface of what can be accomplished with technology and data. Imagine being able to do micro segmentation of the customer data down to an individual level, so that we can offer hyper personalized services and products across channels in real time, at precisely the moment when they are needed. That is the holy grail of the omnichannel experience.

Another promising use case where AI can be helpful is around advisory and personal finance. We need to develop ways to make these services more useful and beneficial for the users, and at the same time, enable monetization in a way that not only benefits the financial institution, but also allows us to reinvest some of the profits back into the society. A rising tide lifts all boats; technology can serve to benefit more people.

What We Can Learn from History

The current AI landgrab reminds me of what we experienced in the past three decades of the internet revolution. At the time of writing this chapter, the US Department of Justice won the lawsuit that it filed against Google in 2020, for monopolistic practices that helped them sustain their dominance in internet search. Back in 1999, a federal judge determined that Microsoft used their dominance of its Windows operating system to force PC manufacturers to include Microsoft's Internet Explorer browser in Windows, and such *power of the default* acted as a barrier of entry where their competitors such as Netscape Navigator were effectively shut out.

In announcing the ruling of the Google antitrust case, Judge Amit Mehta cited the Microsoft case as reference, pointing out that Google's payment to Apple—36% of the Safari search revenue—helped place Google as the default search engine for Apple iPhone users.[26] This gives them an unfair advantage compared to Google's rivals.

In fact, the Google search engine is so dominant that "google" has become synonymous to search. So even if or when Google can no longer be a default search engine on the smartphones, there is a high chance that users will continue to use it by default. How the case will eventually play out remains to be seen, including whether the Justice Department may consider Google to break off part of the company. Meanwhile, additional antitrust charges have also been filed against Apple and Amazon in the past few years, by both US and European Union authorities.

The flurry of actions brings up a question though: Have regulators been too slow to act? And given what we have learned, what may we do differently to prevent control of powerful technologies such as AI, by a handful of big tech companies?

Consider NVIDIA, a dominant player in the AI chip market with 90% market share on the next generation graphics processing units (GPUs) according to GlobalData. Demand soars as AI chatbots become popular in recent years and more powerful hardware is needed to train the large language models that power the likes of ChatGPT. Its market cap has grown considerably as a result, and the tech giant has come under scrutiny due to its sheer dominance. The planned $700 million acquisition of Israeli AI startup, Run:ai, has been delayed, pending review by the Justice Department. Acquisition of a second AI startup, Deci, for $300 million, is also in pending status at the time of writing.

Depending on Google's next step, another potential parallel can be drawn with Gemini Live, Google's AI voice assistant. During my travels in Asia,

I am always fascinated by how often people trade voice memos via WhatsApp. Many has long touted the potential of voice technologies to become the primary way that we interact with our mobile phones, and with each improvement, we are getting closer.

Now imagine Google leveraging similar tactics with Gemini as they did with Google Search, embedding the virtual assistant as the default in their Android operating system for mobile phones and other portable devices, granting it unparalleled access to the data on device. Will the current ruling on search acts as a deterrent against such a move? Or will Google play nice with other virtual assistants to avoid scrutiny by regulators? Only time will tell.

While the private sector may lead in innovating and commercializing ideas, we still need the support of all other stakeholders, including educational institutions and government bodies, to create an environment that can support and grow the technology and the talent.

Together, we can thrive and solve the unsolvable. Divided, we will struggle and face the insurmountable.

Notes

1. How Much Does It Cost to Train Frontier AI Models? EPOCH.AI, 3 June 2024. https://epochai.org/blog/how-much-does-it-cost-to-train-frontier-ai-models
2. S Shead, Why DeepMind co-founder Mustafa Suleyman has quit Google to become a VC, CNBC, Jan 28 2022. https://www.cnbc.com/2022/01/28/mustafa-suleyman-deepmind-co-founder-quits-google-ai-role-to-be-vc.html
3. K Wiggers, Amazon hires founders away from AI startup Adept, Techcrunch, 28 June 2024. https://techcrunch.com/2024/06/28/amazon-hires-founders-away-from-ai-startup-adept/
4. An update on how we're accelerating the use of AI in robotics at scale, Amazon, 30 August 2024. https://www.aboutamazon.com/news/company-news/amazon-covariant-ai-robots
5. M Kruppa and L Thomas, Google Paid $2.7 Billion to Bring Back an AI Genius Who Quit in Frustration, Wall Street Journal, 25 September 2024. https://www.wsj.com/tech/ai/noam-shazeer-google-ai-deal-d3605697

6. B Perrigo, Inside Anthropic, the AI Company Betting That Safety Can Be a Winning Strategy, TIME, 30 May 2024. https://time.com/698 0000/anthropic/

7. US AI Safety Institute Signs Agreements Regarding AI Safety Research, Testing and Evaluation With Anthropic and OpenAI, NIST, 29 August 2024. https://www.nist.gov/news-events/news/2024/08/us-ai-safety-institute-signs-agreements-regarding-ai-safety-research.

8. Evident AI Index Banks: Key Findings Report, Evident AI, October 2024. https://evidentinsights.com/reports/key-findings-rep ort-2024-public?id=f220734de8

9. Government's trailblazing Institute for AI Safety to open doors in San Francisco, Gov.UK, 20 May 2024. https://www.gov. uk/government/news/governments-trailblazing-institute-for-ai-safety-to-open-doors-in-san-francisco.

10. AI perspectives: Transaction fraud, Mastercard, n.d. https://b2b.mas tercard.com/media/5pynmm5n/ai-perspectives-transaction-fraud-sur vey-report.pdf

11. AI Index Annual Report, Stanford University, nd. https://aiindex.sta nford.edu/report/

12. An action plan for artificial intelligence in Australia, Australian Government Department of Industry, Science and Resources, 18 June 2021. https://www.industry.gov.au/news/action-plan-artificial-intellige nce-australia

13. National Artificial Intelligence Centre, Australian Government Department of Industry, Science and Resources, n.d. https://www.ind ustry.gov.au/science-technology-and-innovation/technology/national-artificial-intelligence-centre

14. Funding to establish Artificial Intelligence and Digital Capability Centres, Australian Government, 1 August 2024. https://business.gov. au/grants-and-programs/ai-digital-capability-centres

15. Brazil proposes $4 billion AI investment plan, Reuters, 30 July 2024. https://www.reuters.com/technology/artificial-intelligence/ brazil-proposes-4-billion-ai-investment-plan-2024-07-30/

16. China accelerates AI development to build AI innovation center, The State Council—The People's Republic of China, 6 April 2024. https:// english.www.gov.cn/news/202404/06/content_WS6610834dc6d086 8f4e8e5c57.html

17. The AI Index Report, Stanford University Human-Centered Artificial Intelligence. https://aiindex.stanford.edu/wp-content/uploads/ 2024/04/HAI_AI-Index-Report-2024_Chapter4.pdf

18. Realizing our best tomorrow, Vision 2030, Saudia Data & AI Authority, October 2020. https://ai.sa/Brochure_NSDAI_Summit%20version_EN.pdf

19. D Nair, M Martin, and E Ludlow, Saudis Plan $100 Billion AI Powerhouse to Rival UAE Tech Hub, Bloomberg, 6 November 2024. https://www.bloomberg.com/news/articles/2024-11-06/saudis-plan-100-billion-ai-powerhouse-to-rival-uae-s-tech-hub

20. O Olama, I Was the First AI Minister in History, Time, 19 January 2024. https://time.com/6564430/ai-minister-uae/

21. UAE National Strategy for Artificial Intelligence 2031, United Arab Emirates, Minister of state for artificial intelligence, n.d. https://ai.gov.ae/strategy/

22. UAE National Strategy for Artificial Intelligence 2031, United Arab Emirates, Minister of state for artificial intelligence, n.d. https://ai.gov.ae/strategy/

23. National AI Strategy, GOV.UK, 18 December 2022. https://www.gov.uk/government/publications/national-ai-strategy/national-ai-strategy-html-version

24. The AI Index Report, Stanford Institute for Human-Centered Artificial Intelligence, n.d. https://aiindex.stanford.edu/report/

25. AI Lab, Financial Conduct Authority, 17 October 2024. https://www.fca.org.uk/firms/innovation/ai-lab

26. J Elias and R Goswami, Alphabet pays Apple 36% of Safari search revenue, Sundar Pichai confirms, CNBC,14 November 2023. https://www.cnbc.com/2023/11/14/google-pays-apple-36percent-of-safari-search-revenue-sundar-pichai.html

5

Trust and Evolution of Risk

Trust cannot be assumed.

Where there are people and money, there will be bad actors. Unfortunately, with the evolution of AI, it is getting harder to identify what is real and what is fake. Ultimately, trust is the cornerstone of financial services. When we deposit our hard-earned money in the bank, we trust that we can get it back when needed. When we withdraw cash from the ATMs, we trust that the cash can be exchanged for products and services. When we sign a contract, we trust that the other party is who they claim they are. Without trust, the industry and the society at large will cease to function.

Imagine the internet being flooded with deepfake media designed to mislead people and create public discourse; just like an oil spill that cannot be cleaned up, but with bad data and misinformation.

Only now it can be done even faster, cheaper, and easier. When the customer receives "bad" information from an AI chatbot, whose responsibility is it? When bad actors use AI to exploit unsuspected organizations or individuals, who should pay?

The increased coupling between technology and financial services is quickly transforming the risk landscape as we know it. In this chapter, we will explore what "trustworthiness" entails, the dark age of fraud, and the evolving scope of risk management in financial services. We will also look at some of the promising technology that is helping financial institutions combat the rise of fraud (Fig. 5.1).

© The Author(s), under exclusive license to Springer Nature Switzerland AG 2025
T. Lau, *Banking on (Artificial) Intelligence*, https://doi.org/10.1007/978-3-031-81647-5_5

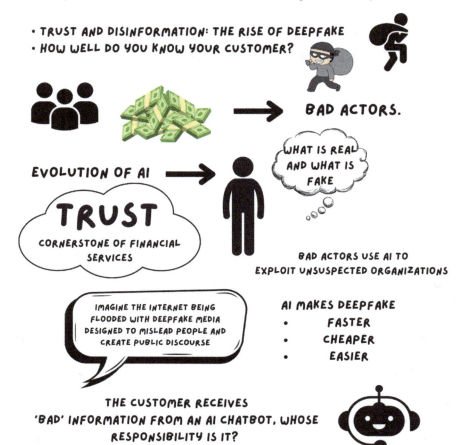

Fig. 5.1 Trust and evolution of risk

Trust and Disinformation

We have spent a great deal of Chapter 4 focusing on the tech industry, and the partnerships between big technology, financial services incumbents, and startups. For my banking friends, you might be wondering: Why does it matter?

I must admit, I am intrigued. Having come from a technology background, I am fascinated at not just the evolution of the technology, but the pace at which things have evolved in the past few years. As an avid reader, I struggle trying to keep up.

But there is a more practical side of the story. It was only a few years ago that the acronym denoting the consumer-facing big platform companies GAFA (Google, Amazon, Facebook, and Apple) was everywhere. The "amazonification" of banking—or the unbundling of banking services—was the buzzword that dominated our industry. We were told that big techs were coming to eat our lunch, service by service, and we must transform—so that we too could provide banking services with an experience as seamless as transacting with Amazon.

Fast forward to 2024. GAFA has evolved to become the Magnificent Seven, comprised of Microsoft, Apple, Tesla, Amazon, Meta, Alphabet, and NVIDIA of the S&P 500. These companies have become prominent torch bearers for AI, an industry that requires substantial resources to operate from. A few trends contribute to the growth and the maturity of the industry, and uniquely position the big tech companies to thrive:

- Availability of data—As we have discussed earlier in the book, having large amount of the right data to train the models is crucial.
- Advances in computational power—To process and analyze the vast amount of data and to drive useful insights out of it requires massive amount of computing power and substantial cloud infrastructure.
- Expanded use cases across sectors—With innovation and new use cases being deployed across sectors, AI adoption increases, which leads to more excitement and subsequently, funding and collaboration, in the industry,

Rising demand not only drives increased and urgent need for data center construction and auxiliary services, a topic that we will go deeper in Chapter 8, but also a tighter collaboration between a wide ecosystem of stakeholders, from academia to government agencies and private sectors. With AI being more deeply embedded in our highly regulated industry, the relevant risks increase as well, especially around the use of data, where the data is being sourced from, how the model is trained, and whom it might impact. Such questions are not trivial, as they can drive undesirable outcomes and harm the most vulnerable population among us.

Duality of AI in Risk and Compliance

Regulatory concern is another prominent risk area that keeps executives up at night. In fact, according to a report from DLA Piper, ensuring that AI initiatives work within regulatory guidelines was one of the top challenges cited by 96% of survey respondent. Nearly half of them have interrupted, paused, or reset an AI initiative due to privacy issues and lack of governance framework.[1]

The potential benefits will likely outweigh the risks from a business perspective, however. After all, as our world continues to evolve, the future belongs to those who can leverage AI effectively in their day-to-day lives. Put it succinctly, we cannot afford to not use AI: the opportunity costs are simply too high. The question is no longer whether we should leverage AI in financial services; but rather, it is where we should start and how do we scale.

While we may be quite familiar with the potential of AI, or generative AI, in augmenting the workforce and driving efficiencies in operations, there is another less discussed opportunity hiding in plain sight: risk and compliance. According to IBM's 2024 research on global banking outlook for banking and financial markets, applying generative AI to address risk and compliance challenges and opportunities top the list of use cases that can deliver the greatest business value.[2]

But this is also where the duality of the technology comes into play.

On one hand, generative AI can help financial institutions create, test, and deploy code, speeding up software development and transformation of legacy banking systems—often faced with tech debt that can severely hinder the ability for incumbent financial institutions to adopt new technologies and adapt to the demands of our changing world. On the other hand, the speed at which generative AI capabilities evolve, and the shorter technology cycles have also introduced operational and regulatory risks to the banking ecosystem, with concerns around lack of transparency into how the large language models operate and how / what data is sourced and used in the training and maintenance of the models. Beyond testing for accuracy and bias, organizations must also consider the legal liability for use of the AI models and the data.

According to the same IBM report, while 86% of banking organizations are in production or preparing to go live with generative AI use cases, only 8% are taking a systemic enterprise-wide approach. How then can banks evolve and become AI-ready throughout the organization and across a broader set of business domains?

The ability for financial institutions to transform is particularly appealing when it comes to capturing the small and medium enterprise market, which forms the backbone of our economy but has traditionally underserved. For small business owners, time is valuable, and every moment counts. And while these small enterprises need access to capital to grow, the finance gap is estimated at $5.7 trillion according to the IFC.[3]

Banks must be able to meet them where they are and when they need—without getting bogged down by the complexity of legacy processes. Unfortunately, they aren't always speaking the same language when it comes to needs and capabilities. According to findings from the report, "Banking for small and medium enterprises", by IBM's Institute for Business Value and Banking Industry Architecture Network (BIAN), with contributions from the IFC, there is a sizeable disconnect between what the banks offer for SME banking services versus what the SMEs need. Beyond the $5.7 trillion SME funding gap, SMEs also pay a credit premium when accessing funding opportunities, due to the complex nature of credit risk assessment with the diverse SMEs market. Breaking down these barriers with data and AI, for example, to enhance credit risk analysis, can help foster growth in a diverse and crucial segment of our society. While getting to full automation of key business processes is still a long-term journey for many financial institutions, it is one that banks nevertheless need to embark on to create value and reduce the cost-to-serve.

Being an AI-Ready Bank

To effectively implementation automation, however, banks must move beyond merely digitizing the analog processes. With AI, banks can now redesign and re-imagine all core business processes—focusing on simplicity and ease of use—and help ensure that human intervention into operations is only required for exceptions and added-value activities. The use case from Casca in Chapter 2 served as a great example on how a community bank and fintech can partner and re-imagine the lending process for small businesses.

Operating model matters as well as the AI capability maturity level within the bank varies. One structure is to have AI architects and experts earmarked for high-profile projects embedded with the business owners. But such silo approach can also create operational and cost inefficiencies since data and machine learning expertise can be hard to find. Instead of spreading the AI experts across different teams, an alternative is a platform model. Such centralized approach with dedicated AI team enables a shared infrastructure and better coordination when developing and deploying solutions, which encourages standards and governance to be established and followed. This can in turn improve efficiencies and reduce risks. Overtime, it also fosters longer term vision and value creation.

Paolo Sironi, who leads the IBM thought leadership research in Banking and Financial Market, offers the following: "An AI-ready bank is an institution in which every banker is an AI risk manager. This allows shifting operations and business models from tactical + AI approaches to strategic AI + operations that can scale enterprise wide with trust." Simply put, we need to go from simply integrating AI into existing processes, to reimagining these processes around AI. Only then can we fully harness the power of emerging technologies and deliver trusted and value-added relationships that are SMEs demand.

Spotlight on Bankwell
Conversation with Ryan Hildebrand, EVP and Chief Innovation Officer. Content has been edited for clarity.

Before banks embark on their AI journey, there are six critical questions that they must ask themselves.

1. What are our strategic goals? AI shouldn't be adopted for its own sake. Clearly define objectives—improved efficiency, enhanced customer experience, new revenue streams, risk mitigation—before selecting AI solutions.
2. Is our data ready, and if not, how are we going to get AI-ready? AI thrives on high-quality, relevant data. Assess the quality, accessibility, and security of existing data assets. Gaps will need to be addressed before effective AI implementation.
3. What are the ethical and regulatory implications? Consider data privacy (GDPR and CCPA), algorithmic bias, transparency, and explainability. Proactive risk management is crucial. Do we have governance around this? What's our policy and procedures?
4. What skills and infrastructure do we need? Strong third-party partners play a crucial role. Even well-positioned banks will have gaps. AI implementation requires technical expertise, (for example, data scientists and engineers), business acumen, and modern infrastructure, including cloud

computing and analytics platforms. Identify skill gaps and invest in upskilling or partnerships.

5. Is our culture ready? AI adoption requires buy-in across the organization and should be led top-down. Effective communication, training, addressing employee concerns, and change management are essential for successful transformation.

6. How will you measure success? Define key performance indicators (KPIs) to track the success of AI initiatives. This ensures accountability and allows for adjustments based on measurable outcomes.

An AI-ready bank has a diverse team who are intellectually curious and willing to experiment, can learn from failures, and adapt quickly. There is a strong data culture in the bank, where data is seen as a valuable asset, not just a byproduct of operations. There must be a robust and scalable cybersecurity and technology infrastructure; protecting sensitive customer data is of paramount importance. Finally, there needs to be a strong governance framework with clear guidelines and processes for responsible AI partnership, development and deployment, and strong third-party risk management.

To move from initial proof-of-concept to long-term deployment, you need to first be able to establish a clear return-on-investment: Quantify the benefits of AI in terms of cost savings, revenue generation, and improved efficiency. You will also need to figure out how to integrate with the core and ancillary products and develop new policies and procedures to ensure smooth operation. Again, risk management is crucial here. Finally, build a strong team by ensuring support and training to team members who are going to be stakeholders in the new solution.

At the start of our AI journey at Bankwell, we ran into data hygiene issues; our data was not clean, and it was kept in various formats, with no single record of truth. This was something that we had not tackled due to technical challenges and time constraints. Finding AI-focused talent, as well as educating existing team members and overcoming inertia and skepticism were also challenging. Not to mention, navigating evolving regulations related to AI and data is complex; at times, there isn't even a roadmap nor policy to follow. As a financial institution, ensuring transparent and explainable AI models for both users and regulators is essential but can be difficult—try to make the decision-making process understandable at the most basic level.

Trust is at the core of our industry. We can build trust in AI through educating consumers and our employees about AI's capabilities and limitations and be transparent about how it works and what data it uses. We must foster communications and keep humans in the loop—to review and make decisions. Fairness is also important when it comes to cultivating trust; ensure the AI treats all customers fairly and does not perpetuate existing biases created in past models. And finally, make sure robust security measures are in place to protect customer data.

As I look toward the future, I am excited about the ability for AI to provide personalized financial advice, especially for small business owners and consumers. Debt refinance opportunities become seamless, and customers win. You can also use AI to optimize your cashflow, to help your business grow or become more efficient; akin to having a CFO in your pocket. Risk management and regulatory compliance will come into focus as AI automates regulatory compliance processes and identifies potential risks, opening up systems to regulators can things much more transparent. And finally, AI can identify and prevent fraudulent transactions in real time instead of days or weeks later.

And here is my prediction: In less than 10 years, I believe we'll have a top 25% bank in the country run by 10 humans or less. It will be the most efficient bank in the country!

Leading with Trust and Expertise

Trust and transparency are paramount in our industry, and especially in an AI-led future. Putting AI to work will require the executive leadership team, not just the CIO, but also the COO and CFO, to be actively involved from the very beginning, actively weighing benefits, risks, and exposures, crafting an enterprise-wide data and AI strategy, defining the success factors and establishing key metrics, in partnership with internal and external stakeholders. New roles, such as Chief AI Officer, Chief Data Officer (CDO), or Chief Ethics Officer, are being created, introducing new responsibilities around governance. NewVantage Partners, for example, who began conducting surveys with senior data leaders from Fortune 1000 companies since 2012, noted that the number of organizations who had a Chief Data Officer or Chief Data & Analytics Officer had jumped from 12 to 82.6%.[4] Having an understanding on how AI works, the key players in the ecosystem, and the dynamics between the stakeholders is crucial, regardless of the size of the organization.

But this brings another layer of obstacle for many organizations: Becoming AI-ready requires time, commitment, and talent. Take the UK and Ireland market for example, where a large portion of businesses envision significant benefits from generative AI, and one in five companies are planning to roll out generative AI at the enterprise level, according to a survey conducted by

Coleman Parkes in 2024 on behalf of SAS on generative AI challenges and potential.[5] However, one in four organizations is finding it challenging to integrate the technology into existing systems. While the reasons are often multifaceted, lack of strategic thinking is likely a significant contributor. Shockingly, almost all (96%) senior decision-makers of technology indicate that they do not fully understand generative AI or its potential impact on the business processes. And fewer than one in 20 organizations provide a high level of training on generative AI governance and monitoring.

Closing this AI literacy gap in the key decision-maker level before developing the AI strategy is the critical first step to ensuring that the organization is embarking on the right path, and that a meaningful return on investment can be delivered.

Lack of expertise can also expose the organization to potential risks including data privacy and security, bias and explainability, as well as compliance and governance. This is where the "move fast and break things" culture in tech industry may need a re-think, especially when it comes to matters that affect highly regulated industries such as financial services, where being quick is not always best. Fear of missing out (FOMO) can lead to organizations rushing to deploy technology before the proper governance and guardrails are in place, leading to reputational risks and erosion of trust. This begs the question: Are small financial institutions more exposed to such challenges as they are likely more dependent on third-party service providers to compete with the bigger institutions?

How concerned should we be of third-party risks influencing the stability of the financial services industry? The collapse of Silicon Valley Bank (SVB), accelerated by the lightning speed at which rumors spread like wildfire on social media platforms, offered a grim example. While bank runs are not new, the speed at which SVB collapsed was: The second largest bank failure happened over the course of merely two days. Succession of tweets by prominent investors and high-profile Silicon Valley entrepreneurs on Twitter caused mass panic, leading to the first bank run fueled by social media, amplified by instant access to digital tools, from mobile phones and banking apps to digital messaging and social media sites. The social media risk was unprecedented; it underscored the power of technology—the speed at which information and misinformation travels that can lead to heightened reputational risk and deposit flight risks. And it serves as a wakeup call for both financial institutions and regulators to develop a more proactive risk management approach—in identifying, assessing, monitoring, measuring, and mitigating the unique related risks brought on by the internet, including social media risks. Whether we like it or not, digital media shape the public's beliefs and expectations; and we must adapt and be prepared to counteract online threats when they occur.

The onus is on those who develop technologies and those who adopt them, to ensure they innovate in a responsible manner, and that the proper guardrails are in place. In Chapters 9 and 10, we will explore the state of regulations on AI in various jurisdictions and concepts on developing responsible and trustworthy AI.

Rise of Fake Content

Apart from the need for talent at the leadership level, cybersecurity is another concern with new data architecture. Here, it is crucial that we take a multi-prong approach toward cybersecurity and fraud detection—one that focuses on both the technical and human factors.

One might argue, fraud is not new. And for as long as technology has been around, we have always experienced bad actors exploiting the vulnerabilities of our systems. While that is true, AI has been increasingly skilled at creating an experience that has made it hard to detect whether it is fake or real. And the speed at which technology can spread disinformation and misinformation with increased sophistication is simply unprecedented. In 2023, an image showing an explosion near the Pentagon spread across social media just after the US stock market opened for trading at 9:30 AM caused a ripple in the market.[6] As it turned out, it was an AI-generated image spread in part by Russian government-sponsored media outlets. This incident serves as a reminder that in today's world, speed can be a blessing and a curse. Unfortunately, with proliferation of algorithmic trading, our system is becoming even more vulnerable to misinformation and disinformation, and exposed to bad actors who may seek to exploit and destabilize the system.

Perhaps it shouldn't come as a surprise that not long after ChatGPT was released, a malicious version of the AI chatbot was made available, for the purpose of helping bad actors generate phishing messages and malware. Known as WormGPT, the generative AI tool can create convincing fake emails that can be used by even novice criminals with limited language fluency. Separately, a known vulnerability in ChatGPT allows hackers to plant false information through prompt injection into ChatGPT's long-term storage of an unsuspected user, causing the LLM to incorporate the false information created by a malicious attacker to steer all future conversations with the target.

Advancements in technology have also made it much easier to create realistic AI-enabled voice and images, to imitate the actual voice pattern and face of individuals. When human voice can be cloned in a matter of seconds, bad actors can potentially use the AI-generated audio to get past the voice authentication, gain access to bank accounts, and transfer assets out of the breached accounts.

According to Cybersecurity Ventures, the global annual cost of cybercrime is expected to reach $9.5 trillion by 2024, or $1 billion an hour.[7] Beyond lost productivity and data theft, such events can cause major disruption to operations as well as reputational harm to the institution.

In February 2024, a finance employee of London-based design and engineering firm, Arup, was duped into believing that he was attending a video call with the Chief Financial Officer and other members of the company. Following instructions from those whom he believed were his colleagues, $25.6 million was sent across multiple transactions.[8] Unfortunately, the attendees from the call turned out to be created from fake voices and images.

The ability to create deepfake content and identity can also make it easier to carry out romance scams, where bad actors use fake identity to gain the trust of their target before exploiting them for money. According to the FTC, in 2023, reported losses to romance scams total $1.14 billion, with median losses at $2000 per person, making this the highest reported losses for imposter scam.[9] And this figure is likely underreported.

While many of these might seem to be isolated incidents, it is not hard to see how things can quickly escalate over time, as technology becomes increasingly sophisticated and affordable. In fact, Deloitte's Center for Financial Services predicted that generative AI could propel fraud losses to US$40 billion in the US alone by 2027—due to the proliferation of malicious software to create deepfake videos, audio, and handwriting.[10] And the damage is not limited to financial losses. In a roundtable hosted by a bipartisan AI Working Group established by the House Committee on Financial Services, a panelist testified that his firm has seen a 450 percent year-over-year increase in deep fake attacks against financial institutions; increasing the prevalence of these incidents, especially if high-profile companies are involved, will risk erosion of trust in financial institutions.[11]

This also brings up the question around accountability—a central theme that you have seen and will continue to see throughout this book. When a victim falls for the scammer and being led to believe that it is true love, what role do and should banks play? While this same question of responsibility exists with or without AI, it is nevertheless an important one, and something that will happen more frequently with increasingly sophisticated technology.

Should banks do more to stop suspicious transfers? The answer is not always a technical one—rather, a question in accountability and responsibility.

Consider the lawsuit against Schwab, filed on behalf of a 92-year-old retired nurse, alleging that while the victim's daughter had asked the firm to intervene, the bank repeatedly ignored the warnings and requests, causing the older woman to lose her life savings to a "computer repair scam".[12]

In another case, scammers edited an interview with Musk by replacing his voice with an AI-generated one with matching mouth movement, advocating for an investment opportunity that promised quick returns. An 82-year-old retiree saw the video, opened an account with the company, and invested more than $690,000 from his retirement funds.[13] Little did he know, it was an AI-powered deepfake-driven scam.

While everyone can fall victim to scams, bad actors often target older adults since they typically own more assets. According to the FBI, older Americans reported losing $3.4 billion in 2023 to fraud, representing an increase of 11% from a year prior.[14]

Fighting AI with AI

As bad actors continue to look for ways to exploit technology, organizations are increasingly using technology, specifically AI and machine learning, to try to stay ahead of the fraudsters. According to the 2024 Anti-fraud technology benchmark report, it is expected that by 2026, half of all organizations expect to use AI and machine learning as part of their fraud analytics initiatives, including physical biometrics (such as fingerprints, face recognition, and voice recognition) and behavioral biometrics. An astonishing 83% of organizations expect to implement generative AI as part of their anti-fraud programs over the next two years—and for good reasons.[15] Deployment of AI and automated security measures can help speed up the identification and containment of vulnerabilities by as much as 108 days.[16]

With fraud methods becoming more sophisticated, financial institutions must also make use of more data types to create a more holistic defense strategy. While structured data that is formatted and predictable may be the easiest to use, unstructured data such as emails and documents often contain insights around human behavior and intention, that can be useful in predicting the intention to commit fraud. With the help of powerful emerging technologies, not only can data analytics be performed more efficiently and accurately, but it can also handle more volume in a shorter amount of time, which helps to uncover trends and patterns.

Speed and adaptability are crucial when it comes to fraud detection. While traditional rules-based monitoring systems are reliable, they are labor intensive to maintain, do not scale well, and cannot adapt quickly to changes. This is where AI can help.

In the case of Bunq, the fast-growing European fintech with over 12 million customers, supervised and unsupervised learning is used to automate its transaction monitoring system and train their fraud detection model. The results are impressive: Using NVIDIA's accelerated computing platform, Bunq can now use larger datasets with hundreds of millions of rows, and train nearly 100 times faster. The increase in processing speed allows the fintech to update their model more frequently, resulting in higher accuracy and less false positives.[17]

The use of AI to fight fraud is not limited to private sector either.

The U.S. Department of Treasury's Office of Payment Integrity, for example, has leveraged machine learning to help prevent and recover over $4 billion in fraud and improper payments in the fiscal year October 2023—September 2024. This represents a huge increase from $652.7 million in the fiscal year prior.[18]

Out of this amount, $1 billion was recovered through implementation for Treasury check fraud identification. The rest came from risk-based screening ($500 million), payment processing efficiency improvement ($180 million), and high-risk transaction identification ($2.5 billion).

To put this in context, the Treasury disbursed 1.4 billion payments valued at over $6.9 trillion dollars to more than 100 million people annually. Being able to leverage data and technology to prevent fraudulent and improper payments is crucial, especially as financial fraud continues to proliferate, with online payment fraud expected to cumulatively surpass $362 billion by 2028 according to Juniper Research. And financial institutions have reported more than $688 million in suspicious activity from February to August 2023 alone, according to FinCEN.[19]

As we discussed in the prior chapter, several factors must be considered before organizations embark on the AI journey. This includes accuracy of the output, security risks, data governance, regulatory concerns, and skillsets.

Spotlight on SAS

Based on conversation with SAS on Enterprise Customer Decisioning. Content has been edited for clarity.

Gone are the days that we can put band-aids on systems to meet changing customer demands while protecting them against fraudsters. As organizations adopt AI, one of the first steps they need to take is to break down the data silos and bring the massive amount of data together so they can make faster, better, and stronger decisions—a concept that SAS calls Enterprise Customer Decisioning. By taking a singular platform approach, organizations can take a broader view across the customer journey, enable a more seamless customer experience, as well as better outcomes for customers.

Think of the typical approach behind-the-scenes when a customer visits a bank website to look for loans. You first need to decide on what to present to the customer and how you want to make it attractive or engaging for them. Then you need to bring them through the application journey, from identity verification, credit risk assessment, fraud assessment, and other due diligence and sanctions screening. Having everything integrated into a single process instead of silos can provide a more seamless customer experience.

The world is more connected with many more players today. Agility and scalability are critical for organizations to stay competitive and create more value for customers. Digital transformation is really a decisioning transformation because it radically changes how banks are making their decisions. As bad actors are increasingly using AI to change their tactics, banks also need to become more proactive and leverage the technology to adapt and become smarter.

With fraud, having third-party data is especially important for predictive modeling, and real time data orchestration as the customer is online or transacting is crucial. With SAS enterprise fraud solution, Techcombank can respond faster to threats and reduce false positives, slashing the time needed for fraud detection to mere seconds. For the number one bank in Vietnam in 2024 with over three hundred branches and 13.8 million customers, this is a huge win.

So how future-ready is your enterprise decisioning architecture?

Seeing but not Believing

Cyber risk is business risk, and a new generation of AI-based cyberattacks is introducing new risks to the environment in unprecedented ways—with the speed, scale, and sophistication not seen before. How best can organizations manage and mitigate the growing risks?

In today's generative AI systems, data is a crucial input, and large amounts of data from different sources are being gathered, analyzed, processed, and stored for the purpose of training and retraining LLMs. It is not a coincidence that data-related challenges are the primary concern for many organizations when it comes to deploying AI effectively. In a SAS study on generative AI in insurance, the top two concerns cited by insurance leaders regarding the use of generative AI are data privacy and data security.[20] In a separate study by NVIDIA, the respondents also cited data issues as it relates to privacy, sovereignty, and disparate locations as the primary challenge for organizations in achieving their AI goals.[21]

Regardless of industry, maintaining data security should be one of the utmost priorities for any organizations in the digital world to reduce the risks of generative AI tools leaking proprietary data due to prompts from external bad actors. Leveraging AI to fight AI is one of the methods that is gaining popularity. AI can analyze large volumes of data and isolate suspicious behavior for follow-up mitigation measures. By training cybersecurity tools that can detect and learn from AI-generated threats, organizations can block and remediate the attacks and can get ahead of the criminals.

Beyond technical solutions, however, it is important to note that awareness and training are equally critical. Ensuring the proper process and procedures are followed, along with educating employees on the safe handling of data, will provide additional layer of protection against data breaches and other malicious acts, much like peeling an onion. Limiting access to critical applications and preventing sensitive data from being copied and pasted into chatbots can also go a long way in helping organizations reduce risks.

At the time of writing this chapter, the EU leads the rest of the world in terms of having formal AI regulations in place. There are, however, a few legislations being proposed in the US that are worth noting.

Take "Content Origin Protection and Integrity from Edited and Deep-faked Media" COPIED Act, for example. According to the senators, the bill, would "set new federal transparency guidelines for marking, authenticating, and detecting AI-generated content, protect journalists, actors, and artists against AI-driven theft, and hold violators accountable for abuses."[22]

In particular:

- It requires the National Institute of Standards and Technology (NIST) to develop guidelines and standards for content provenance information, watermarking, and synthetic content detection.
- It requires providers of AI tools used to generate creative or journalistic content to allow owners of that content to attach provenance information to it and prohibits removing, disabling, or tampering with the content provenance information.
- The bill also prohibits the unauthorized use of creative or journalistic content with provenance information to train AI models or generate AI

content and authorizes the Federal Trade Commission (FTC) and state attorneys general to enforce the bill's requirements and gives individuals the right to sue violators who use their content without permission.

We will dive deeper into governance and regulations in Chapter 9.

While it feels like we are often playing catch-up, this is nevertheless a good step in the right direction when it comes to protecting the rights of artists and journalists. I do wonder how this will work in practical terms considering all the content deals that OpenAI has already inked with various outlets, all the while when the startup is rumored to be transitioning from non-profit to for-profit.

Evolution of Risk Management

While our industry has always faced a variety of risks, what makes things more challenging now is that much of the innovation in financial services is driven by tech companies and startups that are not necessarily familiar with the governance that comes with a highly regulated industry. Dependent on the solution and the institution, multiple third parties from application developers, security firms, cloud providers, core system and infrastructure providers, mobile carriers, and others will be involved—making risk management more complicated.

Adoption of new technologies always takes time—and along with it, evolution on how we evaluate and assess risks. Here, we will look at the NIST AI Risk Management Framework (AI RMF), which has been adopted by organizations in the US and abroad, the MIT AI Risk Repository, and the NSW Artificial Intelligence Assessment Framework.

It is worth noting that unlike the EU AI Act, neither the NIST AI RMF nor its predecessor, the Blueprint for an AI Bill of Rights (AIBOR), are legally binding. Rather, the NIST AI RMF is intended to be a living document that is adaptable to different organizations of all sizes and relies on the cooperation of the tech industry to attain its end goal.

The NIST AI Risk Management Framework

To fulfill the White House Executive Order to develop safe, secure, and trustworthy AI, the National Institute of Standards and Technology (NIST) released NIST-AI-600-1, the Artificial Intelligence Risk Management Framework: Generative Artificial Intelligence Profile in July 2024, as a companion resource for the AI Risk Management Framework (AI RMF 1.0) released in January 2023.[23] The original AI RMF is intended to help organizations incorporate trustworthiness considerations into the design, development, use, and evaluation of AI products and services, with the goal to minimize potential negative impacts of AI systems and maximize positive ones. It provides a structured approach to govern, map, measure, and manage AI risks and develop AI systems in a responsible way, and ensure that they are safe, secure, and trustworthy.

The subsequent release of the Generative AI Profile seeks to define risks that are new to or exacerbated due to the use of generative AI and provides suggested actions to help organizations govern and manage these risks. Some of the risk factors addressed in the framework include hallucinations, representation harms, data memorization, automation bias, model collapse, and intellectual property. The document also highlights the use of "AI Red-teaming", exercises conducted in a controlled environment with AI developers building AI models, to identify flaws of a generative AI model or system.

Since its release, the NIST AI RMF 1.0 has been recognized and adapted worldwide, including for example, the Voluntary AI Safety Standard established by the Commonwealth of Australia in 2024.[24]

How are some of these risk management practices applied in the real world? A great example is model cards, a concept proposed by Google engineers back in 2018 to promote transparency.[25] The model card in Hugging Face for Meta Llama 3.1 for example, provides information such as supported languages, model release date, license information and intended use cases, training data, training time and power consumption, and estimated greenhouse gas emissions, benchmark scores, and strategy to manage trust and safety risks.[26] Such information (and disclosure) encourages transparent reporting, a key component of responsible AI development, and has been adopted by companies including SAS and NVIDIA.

The MIT AI Risk Repository

The MIT AI Risk Repository is a publicly accessible living database of 777 risks extracted from 43 taxonomies, with the goal of providing a centralized repository and a foundation to help academics, innovators, developers, security professionals, regulators, and policymakers understand, audit, and manage a wide range of risks associated with AI.

Two taxonomies are used to categorize the risks. The first one is a casual taxonomy that classifies how, when, and why AI risks occur. The second one is a domain taxonomy that groups AI risks into seven domains, including: discrimination and toxicity, privacy and security, misinformation, malicious actors and misuse, human–computer interaction, socioeconomic and environmental, and AI system safety, failures, limitations. These risk domains are not mutually exclusive as many of them are interconnected.

According to the MIT researchers who developed the repository, while multiple risk frameworks already exist, none are comprehensive enough to cover all the risk subdomains that are included in the database.[27] In fact, on average, the existing risk frameworks address only about 34% of the AI risk subdomains identified in the MIT AI Risk Repository. For anyone who wants an overview of the AI risk landscape or needs a common frame of reference as they develop research, curriculum, and policy, this is a useful guide.

Development in Other Jurisdictions

Beyond the US, there are notable efforts in other jurisdictions as well. In Australia, for example, the New South Wales Government has implemented the NSW Artificial Intelligence Assessment Framework (NSW AIAF) to promote safe and responsible use of AI, which includes governance and oversight, risk management and mitigation, ethics, capability and capacity building, and continuous development.[28] As of March 2022, the AI Assessment Framework is mandatory for all NSW government agencies when designing, developing, deploying, procuring, or using systems that contain AI components, along with the NSW Ethics Policy. The principles include:

1. Community Benefit: AI must prioritize community outcomes, ensuring alignment with laws, minimizing harm, and maximizing benefit.
2. Fairness: Use of AI will be fair, ensuring not to perpetuate bias and inequality by leveraging diverse representative datasets, monitoring performance, and using rigorous data governance.

3. Privacy and Security: Ensure secure, transparent, and compliant data use to preserve public trust.
4. Transparency: The use of AI will be transparent to the people it could impact, providing review mechanisms that allow concerns to be raised and addressed, privacy preserving, cyber secure and ethical.
5. Accountability: Decision-making remains the responsibility of organizations and individuals.

The Changing Role of the Boards in the AI Era

The heightened interest of AI applications is also keeping board members up at night, especially given the potential risk exposure and legal liability to the organization. From mitigating hallucination to maintaining security and privacy, while ensuring transparency and trustworthiness, organizations need to stay one step ahead. This requires board members (and company executives) to become more familiar with the technology, understand from a high level how and where it is being used, know what questions to ask, and ensure that the necessary controls or gates are in place, so they can better understand and assess the risks and opportunities that AI can enable. A few questions come to mind:

- What problem are we trying to solve? Be clear why AI is the best solution to the problem. And FOMO isn't one of them.
- Where is AI deployed? Some of the lower hanging fruits include customer service chatbots, documentation review and summary generation, knowledge management, and trend analysis. Whereas applications used to detect fraud and determine credit worthiness will need more stringent governance and transparency to mitigate potential risks and safeguard consumer well-being.
- What are the key risk focus areas and in particular, which ones are the ones that will most likely increase in priority? Credit risk management, anti-money laundering, and regulatory compliance are some of the most common areas to consider.
- Can the output be explained to the stakeholders, including regulators? Are there plans in place to proactively engage with regulators to better establish standards in reporting, for example?
- How are the risk teams identifying, managing, and communicating risks? And how do they assess new risks as they arise? Who is accountable—or where does the buck stop so to speak?

- And finally, do the board and the executive team have the right skillset? Does the organization have the right talent and culture to be AI-ready?

Despite potential risks, however, simply staying away from AI to avoid risks is not the smart strategy either, as AI plays an outsized role in transforming the organization into a future-ready one, with the agility and scalability to meet the demands of tomorrow. Leaders have the responsibility to ensure that innovation and development is done responsibly—by having the right strategy and controls in place, with the right talent, governance structure, and use case.

"Avoiding risk isn't risk management. Real risk management is proactive and forward looking, embracing innovation while managing threats intelligently," commented Sajid Iqbal, Vice President of Risk Management, Habib Bank AG Zurich.

As the saying goes, we are all risk managers. The biggest risk of AI is not taking the risk at all.

A Double-Edged Sword

We are at a critical juncture in technology development. In the digital era, time is of essence when it comes to fraud detection. We also need to keep a low false positive while keeping the customers' assets safe and not breaking their trust. Getting to an optimal mix of user experience and fraud prevention is easier said than done. We can't have too much friction that will deter usage and growth; but we also need to have the proper guardrails in place to protect consumers against fraud.

We must also be mindful of the competitive pressure on banks and fintechs to keep up—while the fear of missing out on AI application deployment is real and can be overwhelming, as an industry, we need to be aware of the potential risks to the customers and brand reputation, as well as to the overall financial stability of our society, if we don't have the right controls in place. After all, AI is more than a plug and play technology; it can transform how we serve, who we serve, and how we make decisions at every crossroad. While we might be starting with lower risk use cases, the risks and the potential for negative consequences will continue to evolve as our implementation become more complex and AI is embedded in more aspects of our lives.

Managing AI risks is a work-in-progress. It is time to embrace the change.

Spotlight on conversation with Jas Randhawa, CEO and Managing Partner of StrategyBRIX

Based on conversation with Jas Randhawa. Content has been edited for clarity.

There is a fundamental difference between risk and compliance when it comes to how it is being treated in financial services. In a financial institution, fraud prevention is typically viewed as a business function that impacts the bottom line and exposes the organization to potential financial losses and reputation damage. Here, one of the main drivers is cost savings—the more fraud you can prevent and the faster you can do it, the better it is for the financial institution. On the other hand, compliance is a function that is generally led by Chief Compliance Officer, who reports to either the chief executive officer or the chief legal officer, in addition to maintaining a parallel reporting relationship to the board of directors. The CCO is most concerned about having the proper controls in place to prevent illegitimate transactions and to ensure compliance with regulations, which are written based on if/when rules that require human compliance officers to explain and demonstrate compliance to the examiners.

This is where the challenge lies. While machine learning can detect potential risks proactively more efficiently and at a lower cost due to the sheer volume of data, it is not always possible to explain how the model behaves, especially when modeling techniques and algorithms become increasingly complex, and the model evolves with new data. From a compliance perspective, explainability and transparency are crucial to demonstrate how decisions are made, and to satisfy regulatory requirements when issues arise. Lack of (or limited) reproducibility can expose the financial institution to non-compliance risks and fines.

That said, there are lower risk areas where machines can be helpful, especially when it comes to analyzing and summarizing documents. Automating such mundane tasks can help save time for the compliance professionals, so they can focus on what they do best: Make decisions.

With such operational efficiency gains, we may see up to 70% or 80% compliance workforce reduction in the next five to six years. It is important to remember, however, that while we are becoming more digital, we are not replacing human intelligence with machines; we are merely helping humans make more informed decisions based on data.

Notes

1. DLA Piper Study: Success Factors & Pitfalls for the Use of Artificial Intelligence, n.d. https://www.dlapiper.com/en-us/news/2023/10/dla-piper-study-success-factors-and-pitfalls-for-the-use-of-artificial-intelligence
2. 2024 Global Outlook for Banking and Financial Markets, IBM, 29 January 2024. https://www.ibm.com/thought-leadership/institute-business-value/en-us/report/2024-banking-financial-markets-outlook
3. MSMEs, IFC Financial Institutions Group, n.d. https://www.ifc.org/content/dam/ifc/doc/2024/msme-s-factsheet-ifc-financial-institutions-group.pdf
4. 2024 Data and AI Leadership Executive Survey, Wavestone, January 2024. https://wwa.wavestone.com/app/uploads/2023/12/DataAI-ExecutiveLeadershipSurveyFinalAsset.pdf
5. Generative aI challenges and potential unveiled: How to achieve a competitive advantage, n.d. https://www.sas.com/en_gb/offers/generative-ai-reports.html
6. P Marcelo, FACT FOCUS: Fake image of Pentagon explosion briefly sends jitters through stock market, Associated Press, 23 May 2023. https://apnews.com/article/pentagon-explosion-misinformation-stock-market-ai-96f534c790872fde67012ee81b5ed6a4
7. Cybersecurity Ventures, "Cybercrime Damages To Cost The World $9.5 Trillion USD in 2024", 13 December 2023. https://www.einpresswire.com/article/674883055/cybercrime-damages-to-cost-the-world-9-5-trillion-usd-in-2024
8. K Magramo, British engineering giant Arup revealed as $25 million deepfake scam victim, CNN, 17 May 2024. https://www.cnn.com/2024/05/16/tech/arup-deepfake-scam-loss-hong-kong-intl-hnk/index.html
9. L Fair, "Love Stinks" – when a scammer is involved, Federal Trade Commission, 13 February 2024. https://www.ftc.gov/business-guidance/blog/2024/02/love-stinks-when-scammer-involved
10. Generative AI is expected to magnify the risk of deepfakes and other fraud in banking, Deloitte Center for Financial Services, 29 May 2024. https://www2.deloitte.com/us/en/insights/industry/financial-services/financial-services-industry-predictions/2024/deepfake-banking-fraud-risk-on-the-rise.html.
11. AI Innovation Explored: Insights into AI Applications in Financial Services and Housing, House Committee on Financial Services,

18 July 2024. https://democrats-financialservices.house.gov/uploadedf
iles/07.18.2024__ai_report_final.pdf

12. D Patta, J Axelrod, A Bast, S Samu, J Guzman, and S Carter, Inside the "hustle kingdom," where overseas scammers prey on Americans online, CBS News, 24 September 2024. https://www.cbsnews.com/romancesc ams/

13. S Thompson, How 'Deepfake Elon Musk' Became the Internet's Biggest Scammer, New York Times, 14 August 2024. https://www.nyt imes.com/interactive/2024/08/14/technology/elon-musk-ai-deepfake-scam.html

14. FBI Releases 2023 Elder Fraud Report with Tech Support Scams Generating the Most Complaints and Investment Scams Proving the Costliest, FBI, 2 May 2024. https://www.fbi.gov/contact-us/field-offices/losangeles/news/fbi-releases-2023-elder-fraud-report-with-tech-support-scams-generating-the-most-complaints-and-investment-scams-proving-the-costliest

15. 2024 Anti-Fraud Technology Benchmarking Report, ACFE and SAS, 13 February 2024. https://www.sas.com/en_us/news/press-releases/2024/february/acfe-anti-fraud-tech-study-generative-ai.html

16. IBM Report: Half of Breached Organizations Unwilling to Increase Security Spend Despite Soaring Breach Costs, IBM, 24 July 2023. https://www.prnewswire.com/news-releases/ibm-report-half-of-bre ached-organizations-unwilling-to-increase-security-spend-despite-soa ring-breach-costs-301883346.html

17. A Lee, Digital Bank Debunks Financial Fraud With Generative AI, NVIDIA, 3 June 2024. https://resources.nvidia.com/en-us-financial-services-industry/digital-bank-debunks-financial-fraud

18. Treasury Announces Enhanced Fraud Detection Processes, Including Machine Learning AI, Prevented and Recovered Over $4 Billion in Fiscal Year 2024, U.S. Department of the Treasury, 14 October 2024. https://home.treasury.gov/news/press-releases/jy2650

19. FinCEN Issues In-Depth Analysis of Check Fraud Related to Mail Theft, FinCEN, 9 September 2024. https://www.fincen.gov/news/news-releases/fincen-issues-depth-analysis-check-fraud-related-mail-theft

20. Your journey to a GenAI future: An insurer's strategic path to success, SAS, 2024. https://www.sas.com/en/whitepapers/your-journey-to-a-genai-future-an-insurers-strategic-path-to-success-114043.html

21. State of AI in Financial Services, NVIDIA, 2024. https://www.nvidia.com/en-us/industries/finance/ai-financial-services-report/

22. Cantwell, Blackburn, Heinrich Introduce Legislation to Increase Transparency, Combat AI Deepfakes & Put Journalists, Artists & Songwriters Back in Control of Their Content, U.S Senate committee on commerce, science, & transportation, 11 July 2024. https://www.commerce.senate.gov/2024/7/cantwell-blackburn-heinrich-introduce-legislation-to-combat-ai-deepfakes-put-journalists-artists-songwriters-back-in-control-of-their-content

23. NIST Trustworthy and Responsible AI, National Institute of Standards and Technology, July 2024. https://nvlpubs.nist.gov/nistpubs/ai/NIST.AI.600-1.pdf

24. Voluntary AI Safety Standard, Australian Government, Department of Industry, Science and Resources, 5 September 2024. https://www.industry.gov.au/publications/voluntary-ai-safety-standard.

25. M Mitchell, Model Cards for Model Reporting, Cornell University, 5 October 2018. https://arxiv.org/abs/1810.03993

26. Meta Llama-3.1-8B, Hugging Face, n.d. https://huggingface.co/meta-llama/Llama-3.1-8B

27. K Wiggers, MIT researchers release a repository of AI risks, TechCrunch, 14 August 2024. https://techcrunch.com/2024/08/14/mit-researchers-release-a-repository-of-ai-risks/

28. NSW Artificial Intelligence Assessment Framework, NSW Government, n.d. https://www.digital.nsw.gov.au/policy/artificial-intelligence/nsw-artificial-intelligence-assessment-framework

6

Representation Matters

Talent is everywhere; opportunity is not.

Continuing the theme from Chapter 5, what happens when we can no longer trust what we see and hear? How can we verify one's identity if everything can be forged?

With high volume of data from a wider variety of sources being used in increasingly complex models, financial institutions and fintechs must ensure that proper controls are in place to ensure compliance, privacy, and security, to look for errors and biases in the data that might lead to unintentional consequences, and to ensure adequate protection when it comes to receiving or sharing data with external parties for data modeling.

Where data intelligence is our future, the outcomes are not predetermined. Beyond the quality of data, who is at the decision-making table also matters. Where diverse perspectives and lived experiences are not included, bias across our society and historically will persist and be present in algorithms used in AI systems—where decisions are now automated (Fig. 6.1).

© The Author(s), under exclusive license to Springer Nature
Switzerland AG 2025
T. Lau, *Banking on (Artificial) Intelligence*, https://doi.org/10.1007/978-3-031-81647-5_6

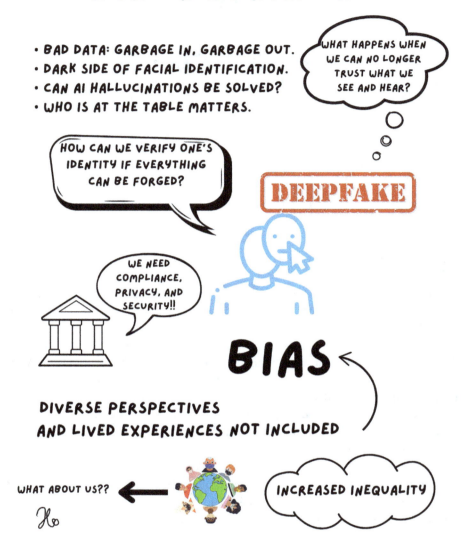

Fig. 6.1 Representation matters

Garbage In, Garbage Out

If algorithm is the beating heart of AI, the data is the lifeblood that powers it. Without good useable data, AI cannot learn effectively, and we will not be able to make better decisions with the tools. As AI becomes more embedded in our daily lives, ensuring that it is aligned with our core values is critical.

Without intentional effort, our data ecosystems will mimic and amplify the inequalities that exist in our society today, enabling groups with access to resources even more opportunities to extract value from the digital economy. This will create further division between the haves and the have-nots in our society.

While such outcome is not inevitable, it will require significant collaboration amongst all stakeholders, including private sectors and policymakers, to create fairer and safer data ecosystems for all. What does this mean and how can we get there?

Can You Hear Me Now?

A decade ago, smart speakers topped everyone's holiday wish lists and home appliances were in a hurry to become voice enabled. Shortly before that, the movie "Her" was released, depicting a story in which a man fell in love with Samantha, and AI virtual assistant with a female-sounding voice. One might argue that none of these voice assistants have an actual gender per se; after all, we are now able to customize the voice, including the gender and accent. You may ask, does it truly matter that these devices (and programs) are typically defaulted to female voices?

I think it does.

How technology behaves is often a reflection of how our world operates, including gender stereotypes. It is also a reflection of their creators, for example, the engineers who code them. When we start to interact with these virtual assistants in ways that we start to humanize them, it is not hard to see how the cultural or social norms get reinforced.

How these devices are trained impact how they perform in real life. I have always joked that our smart devices at home do not understand me—they either confuse what I say, or they just outright ignore me. And often times, I find myself adapting to a different way of speaking just to get the device to respond. It seems counterintuitive though. After all, isn't the voice assistant's primary job to hear/understand and respond? It's one thing if I am asking Siri to set a kitchen timer. It's yet another (and more serious), if I am asking the device to show me how to navigate a route while I am driving.

As with almost everything, there is a technical explanation; and it has to do with the dataset that these speech recognition systems are trained on. If the training data is diverse and rich with audio samples with different accents, dialects, and speaking styles, the model will have an easier time recognizing what the user is saying. Conversely, the performance will be subpar if the model is not exposed to sufficient diversity in the audio training data.

Even though the quality has substantially improved in the past few years, I do still struggle with some of the AI meeting notetakers from time to time. With speech recognition technology becoming more embedded in applications from automatic translation, voice dictation, and video subtitling, to customer service and ordering, it is imperative that we invest in improving the technology so that more people from different backgrounds can benefit from it.

And in some situations, it is not sufficient that it works part of the time. Take healthcare transcripts for example. Can doctors rely on the notes generated from an AI-powered transcription tool if it is only accurate part of the time and it is prone to making up chunks of text or sentences? It is one thing if it's closed caption for a casual interview and a human can go back and validate the content from a video recording; it's another thing (and more serious) when a doctor is using the tool to transcribe a consultation with patients and the doctors cannot access the original recordings for verification.[1] Imagine the potential risks and grave consequences for misdiagnosis. Whose responsibility, is it? The tool developer? Or the doctor?

I've had my share of challenges with such transcription tools for video interviews that I have conducted over the past year—especially when it involves interviewing guests with accents—even slight accents. And I have found myself wasting hours to correct the transcripts, even though I can clearly hear and understand what the speaker is saying but the program cannot. On quite a few occasions, I think that it would have been easier to hire a human to transcribe than use a machine!

This challenge is amplified as we consider the role that AI will play in our not-too-distant future, where the lack of representation becomes more than a mere nuisance, but rather, an economic obstacle as not everyone will be able to fully participate in the AI-led digital economy. Existing large language models are predominantly trained using data from Western cultures and English-speaking countries. Some might argue that this makes sense from a business perspective for a nascent technology that is still being explored, since there is more online data written in English that can be used to train the models, and starting with use cases for demographics that are most likely to adopt the technology can help prove out the concept while testing out the different commercially viable models. However, at the same time, we must have a pathway to start bringing the rest of the communities so that they are not left behind.

If we have established that an AI-enabled future is unavoidable, then equitable access cannot—and must not—be an afterthought. The question is, whose responsibility, is it?

Linguistic diversity is more than just translating the words from one language to another. Cultural context also dictates the vocabulary used and the grammatical rules. In the Chinese language for example, we have different ways of saying the word "aunt", dependent on which side of the family (maternal or paternal), if the aunt is older or younger, if they are related by birth or marriage, and what degree / how far removed they are. As such, the term that I would use to call my mom's older sister, is different than the term I would use to call my mom's younger sister, which is also different than the term that I would use to call my mom's younger brother's wife. The word "rice" is another interesting example. In the Chinese language, cooked rice is represented differently as a singular character, compared to uncooked rice. But in English, it is all the same: rice.

Such complexity and cultural context exist in other languages as well and must be included when we try to create a meaningful representation of diversity in language technology.

But therein lies the problem. Take the African continent as an example—with an estimated 1 billion people in 54 countries. [2] According to the GSMA, there are 2650 times more content available in English on the internet, compared to African languages.[3] In fact, none of the top 34 languages used on the Internet globally is African.[4] Simply put, for people living in Africa, unless you speak English or one of the other major European languages, you will likely not be able to use any of the digital products, including online learning.

With limited content available online in African languages, building local language datasets can be difficult, especially since additional data that can be used to build AI solutions exist in various formats: structured data in standard formats that can be captured relatively easily, or unstructured data in the forms of text, audio, and graphics, that may exist digitally or in hand-written formats. The challenge is further compounded since women in Africa are historically underrepresented in datasets. Without sufficient data, it is difficult to create a model that can accurately represent the realities of women in Africa, thus potentially subjecting them to further algorithmic biases and deepening existing inequalities.

A separate report published by the World Economic Forum revealed a similar struggle with most commercially available models—resulting in subpar results for those who live in less well-off economies.[5]

Data Equity

This brings us to the concept of data equity. Loosely defined, it refers to a shared responsibility to create a more equitable world where data-centric systems promote fair, just, and beneficial outcomes for people and communities, and equitable access to resource and social and economic opportunities. It is concerned about access to datasets, as well as how the data is used and by whom, the impact of data practices, and how the value created is shared. It serves as a foundation of fairness in application and technology development.

The World Economic Forum has developed a data equity framework for reference, modeled after the Te Mana o te Raraunga, which is used to inform the Māori Data Sovereignty Network, and ensure that Māori rights and interests in data can be safeguarded and protected in the increasingly digital world.[6] The framework includes ten data equity characteristics grouped into three main categories: data (sensitivity and accessibility), purpose (application, originality, value, and trust), and people (responsibility, accountability, expertise, and relationship). From input stage (with data collection and curation), through the process stage, and onto the output stage (including data sharing, reuse, and retention), the framework seeks to address the historical, current, as well as future imbalances in datasets that are used in various data-driven decisions and algorithmic and AI systems.

For example, at the beginning of the data lifecycle while the data is being collected and curated, an applicable question would be: Is the data representative of everyone that the system will impact? And has it been assessed for bias, toxicity, and harmful representation? And at the output stage, another applicable question would be: Is the data being shared across borders, and in a safe and secure manner? And what data is stored and for how long?

To put this in context, we can consider a real-world example: Analyzing women's access to formal financial services in emerging economies. At the beginning of the data lifecycle, we may need to increase women's representation in the data set, since gender disaggregated data may not be readily available, and data on informal economy (where women contribute) may not be included. At the processing stage, we need to check credit algorithms for potential bias (since algorithms may be embedded with bias from historical data). And finally at the output stage, we need to regularly assess the performance of the algorithm to minimize bias.

In essence, data equity is an important tenant of responsible innovation, and it must be considered from the initial stage of the data lifecycle and through the end—to minimize inequitable practices and adverse outcomes.

To borrow the words from Iain Brown, Head of Data Science at SAS: "In the orchestra of AI, data scientists are the conductors, harmonizing data, algorithms, and insights to create beautiful symphonies of knowledge." And in this brave new world where data scientists are the unsung heroes who keep the engine running, data equity serves as the foundation of the musical composition.

The Humans of AI

Good news is, there are unsung heroes in many parts of the world and there is reason for hope. Here are some of the efforts that have sprung up to preserve linguistic diversity:

- Recognizing the potential challenges ahead and the cultural significance of language inclusion, part of Brazil's government push for an AI investment plan explicitly stated the goal of developing Portuguese-language AI models to reflect Brazil's cultural and linguistic heritage, as described in Chapter 4.
- India is also taking a similar approach with BharatGen—a generative AI initiative to develop a suite of foundational models in language, speech, and computer vision, that is specifically tailored for India using India-centric data. The press article also specifically called out the need to capture the nuances and diversity of Indian languages, dialects, and cultural contexts, which are often underrepresented in global datasets due to limited digital presence.[7]
- Elsewhere, on 7th February 2024, the European Commission set up the Alliance for Language Technologies under the umbrella of the European Digital Infrastructure Consortium, otherwise known as the ALT-EDIC. The ALT-EDIC counts seventeen member states and eight observing member states within the EU, with the goal of creating a common European data infrastructure and services for language technologies. By consolidating the language data across the EU and its member states, the alliance seeks to promote the development of new LLMs projects and foundation models with robust multilingual and multimodal capabilities.[8] There are 24 official languages represented in the EU. In total, Europe has about 255 living languages, compared to about 2165 in Asia.

- EuroLLM is another project co-funded by the European Union, focusing on building a suite of open source LLMs capable of understanding and generating text in all 24 official languages in the EU, in addition to additional relevant languages, including Arabic, Catalan, Chinese, Galician, Hindi, Japanese, Korean, Norwegian, Russian, Turkish, and Ukrainian.[9]
- To overcome the linguistic barriers for low resource non-Latin languages, Alibaba developed SeaLLMs, a suite of specialized language models that are optimized for Southeast Asian languages, including Burmese, Khmer, Lao, Malay, Tamil, and Thai. The goal is to enable more inclusive access and better performance for languages that are typically not well represented in the digital economy.[10]
- In 1960, only one in four Māori spoke Te Reo Māori, the language spoken by New Zealand's indigenous Māori people. Te Hiku, a tribal-based non-profit media organization founded in 1990, built an audio-visual archive of Māori words, phrases, and idioms and disseminated the language and culture via New Zealand's radio stations and broadcasting services. And in 2017, the team built an open-source app, Kōrero Māori, to collect oral recordings to be used to train computers to understand spoken languages using machine learning.[11] This enables the team to use the model to automatically transcribe thousands of hours of te reo Māori archives previously recorded and develop their first speech-to-text systems.[12]
- In September 2024, OpenAI released a multilingual dataset named Multilingual Massive Multitask Language Understanding (MMMLU) that covers 14 languages, including Arabic, Bengali, German, Spanish, French, Hindi, Indonesian, Italian, Japanese, Korean, Brazilian Portuguese, Swahili, Yoruba, and Simplified Chinese.[13] The dataset is published on Hugging Face, the open data platform, and it aims to fill in some of the gaps in AI research where low-resource languages spoken by millions are left behind.

Notably, OpenAI leverages human translators rather than machines to create the MMMLU dataset, to provide a more reliable foundation and avoid the potential pitfalls with automatic translation tools. This makes a lot of sense as I think we may have all witnessed some of the errors with machine translated text.

Beyond being a melting pot of linguistic diversity, communities are also a hotbed of innovative ideas. But researchers and educators need access to computing power and datasets to conduct their research, develop AI applications, and train the next generation. Here, collaborative efforts between government and private sectors show promise.

- In the UK, the FCA has established the AI Lab to help promote responsible development of AI technologies. Amongst the initiative is a supercharged digital sandbox infrastructure to support AI-focused tech sprints to enable firms to collaborate and experiment.
- In the US, the National Science Foundation (NSF) is leading a pilot effort, called the NAIRR Pilot, in collaboration with federal agencies and non-governmental partners, to connect researchers and educators to AI tools and resources needed to advance trustworthy AI research and spur innovation.[14] This shared infrastructure will aim to provide advanced computational, data, software, training, and educational resources for AI research and education.

There are also other community-led efforts that are worth mentioning and truly inspirational—especially given how experts from some demographics groups have traditionally been underrepresented.

- Dr Joy Buolamwini, a renowned AI researcher who was motivated by her own experiences of algorithmic discrimination, launched the Algorithmic Justice League (AJL) in 2016. While working on a graduate school project at MIT, she found out that the facial analysis software struggled to detect her face, while her peers with lighter skin color did not encounter the same issue. However, when she put a white mask over her face, the machine recognized it immediately. Upon further research, she came upon more gender and skin type biases in commercially sold facial recognition technologies. And this started her journey with AJL, which is committed to advocating for equitable and accountable AI.
- Given the urgent need to ensure women's voices are included in the development of AI, and to shine a spotlight on talented women in the space, Mia Shah-Dand, Founder of Lighthouse3, launched Women in AI Ethics—and along with it, the first publication of "100 Brilliant Women in AI Ethics", to highlight the hidden figures, pioneers, and rising stars from diverse backgrounds.[15]

These efforts represent an important step in the right direction and showcase the power of community and intention. I hope the momentum will continue. As more economies continue to adopt AI, we must provide solutions that can help people from different corners of the world, including and especially the emerging markets, understand and engage with it. And it is becoming more pressing with time.

Where Intention Drives Outcome

As much as we'd like for our system to be bias-free, I do wonder, is it even possible or is it simply a fool's errand?

Since humans are the ones who train the algorithms with real world data, it makes sense that the algorithms will absorb the biases from our real world and potentially reinforce them. The CFPB has made it clear that the use of AI is considered a violation of the Equal Credit Opportunity Act (ECOA), if the lender cannot explain an adverse outcome in credit decisioning by AI.[16] In other words, just because a financial institution is using AI to automate decisions do not absorb them of liability.

As with any high-risk automated decisioning, AI is merely a tool to assist or supplement human decision-making. In the end, humans decide on the outcome. Providing an option for consumers to appeal and discuss the outcome with a human will also go a long way in instilling trust in the system and ensuring that it is working properly. And the feedback loop is crucial, as there are now different solutions in the marketplace that enable lenders to double check and find alternative underwriting models to increase approval rates—which can potentially help extend credit access for borrowers who have historically been denied credit with the more traditional way of assessing creditworthiness and approval thresholds.

According to research from Fairplay, a fintech that focuses on "fairness-as-a-service" solutions, using Less Discriminatory Alternatives (LDA)—lending algorithms that can improve fair lending but with less discriminatory impact on protected classes—can increase approval rates for Black and Hispanic mortgage applicants 5 to 13%, with no increase in risk.[17]

In talking to different colleagues while researching for the book, compliance remains a hot topic issue, especially when it comes to the use of AI in credit decisioning. And I am encouraged by good humans such as Kareem Saleh, Founder and CEO at Fairplay, who is relentlessly focused on financial inclusion, and whose lived experience has helped influence his career path. As this team at Fairplay has shown us, promoting fairness and increasing the bottom line do not have to be mutually exclusive; we can use AI to change the status quo and improve the outcome for historically underrepresented groups—if we are intentional.

Spotlight on Stratyfy
Based on conversation with Deniz Johnson, COO at Stratyfy. Content has been edited for clarity.

Stratyfy was founded in 2017 by Laura Kornhauser and Dmitry Lesnik. When Laura and Dmitry first met, they were both looking for ways to make better predictions, without the need to make trade-offs between accuracy and transparency. Stratyfy was born from this new vision to AI-based decision-making, where AI-enabled data insights and human understanding can be combined to embrace the complexity of how important decisions really need to be made. Our belief is that highly accurate and interpretable AI should be the standard in financial services, because it is what all customers and institutions deserve.

When we talk about responsible AI, it should not be a discussion on AI ethics. While ethics provides a framework, we need to talk about the impact to the bottom line to fuel action. Responsible AI in financial services is precisely that: it is about understanding and making informed decisions that you can explain, not because it was always done that way, but because it is the best decision *both* ethically and financially.

There will always be bias in our decisions. It is simply human nature, and it is part of our culture. While we can never be free of bias, however, it is crucial for us to understand when biases and prejudices are present in our decisions so we can address them thoughtfully. Else, we risk limiting what innovation in technology, especially AI, can do for our society.

Looking forward, we believe that more regulations around the use of AI in financial services will be coming. In the long run, we will see a convergence of multiple disciplines and technologies; maybe we will stop calling it AI or fintech. We will see increased adoption of easy-to-implement AI solutions in financial services and a shift to a more nimble and accessible approach, without the need of large data science teams managing different models. But getting there will require inquisitive users who are willing to learn and to challenge the status quo, instead of taking things at face value. This will go a long way in enabling responsible use of AI and other technologies.

While an AI-led future is inevitable, we still have control over the outcome and the type of society we will live in. For more economies to be included as part of this future and to benefit from the innovations that AI enables, who is at the table matters. In the next two chapters, we will continue exploring the other critical elements for inclusive innovation.

- Affordable access to compute and sufficient capacity
- Talent with digital skills and literacy, as well as resources to build AI skills, and to upskill and reskill future workers
- Supportive regulatory environment that promotes responsible innovation and ethical development of AI

Spotlight on Nicole Königstein, Chief AI Officer and Head of AI & Quantitative Research at Quantmate

Based on conversation with Nicole Königstein. Content has been edited for clarity.

Is the future open source?

It's a nuanced question, but I think that's where we are heading. I have seen banks building their own large language models on top of open source (such as Llama 3.1) and using them on premise or cloud. Beyond being more cost-effective, this is also less risky because you own your tech stack. And I think it is a good trend for the industry to be more distributed, and open source enables people from around the world to collaborate.

Meta, for instance, has contributed a lot to the open-source community. PyTorch, a fully featured framework for developing deep learning models, is the work of Facebook developers and released to open source in 2017. It is easy to use, and it is well-supported by a large and vibrant community with a large collection of tools and libraries. PurpleLlama is a collection of different models to help the community build responsibly with open generative AI models, and the project includes a cybersecurity benchmark. Finally, one of their latest models, SAM 2, is a top-notch model for image segmentation and video segmentation. The entire code is accessible online via their publicly available repository.[18]

Notes

1. G Burke and H Schellmann, Researchers say an AI-powered transcription tool used in hospitals invents things no one ever said, AP, 26 October 2024. https://apnews.com/article/ai-artificial-intelligence-health-business-90020cdf5fa16c79ca2e5b6c4c9bbb14
2. How many Countries in Africa? Worldometer, n.d. https://www.worldometers.info/geography/how-many-countries-in-africa/
3. E Humeau and T Deshpande, AI for Africa: Use cases delivering impact, GSMA, July 2024. https://www.gsma.com/solutions-and-impact/connectivity-for-good/mobile-for-development/wp-content/uploads/2024/07/AI_for_Africa.pdf
4. Solve the African language problem for inclusive AI development, The UN agency for digital technologies, 4 June 2024. https://www.itu.int/hub/2024/06/solve-the-african-language-problem-for-inclusive-ai-development/

5. AI for Impact: The PRISM Framework for Responsible AI in Social Innovation, The World Economic Forum, June 2024. https://www3.weforum.org/docs/WEF_AI_for_Impact_Prism_Framework_2024.pdf

6. Advancing Data Equity: An Action-Oriented Framework, World Economic Forum, 11 September 2024. https://www3.weforum.org/docs/WEF_Advancing_Data_Equity_2024.pdf

7. A Raja, BharatGen: World's First Government-Funded Multimodal LLM Initiative Launched in India, India AI, 1 October 2024. https://indiaai.gov.in/article/bharatgen-world-s-first-government-funded-mul timodal-llm-initiative-launched-in-india

8. Alliance for Language Technologies EDIC, European Commission, n.d.https://language-data-space.ec.europa.eu/related-initiatives/alt-edi c_en

9. P Martins, P Fernandes, J Alves, N Guerreiro, R Rei, D Alves, J Pombal, A Farajian, M Faysse, M Klimaszekski, P Colombo, B Haddow, J Souza, A Birch, A F., T Martins, EuroLLM: Multilingual Language Models for Europe, arXiv, 24 September 2024. https://arxiv.org/abs/2409.16235

10. SeaLLMs-v3 Large Language Models for Southeast Asia, Hugging Face, https://huggingface.co/SeaLLMs/SeaLLMs-v3-7B-Chat

11. Kōrero Māori on your mobile, n.d. https://koreromaori.com/

12. ITU News, How AI is helping revitalize indigenous languages, The UN agency for digital technologies, 9 August 2022. https://www.itu.int/hub/2022/08/ai-indigenous-languages-maori-te-reo/

13. Multilingual Massive Multitask Language Understanding (MMMLU), Hugging Face, n.d. https://huggingface.co/datasets/openai/MMMLU

14. National Artificial Intelligence Research Resource Pilot, n.d. https://nairrpilot.org/about

15. Women in AI Ethics, n.d. https://womeninaiethics.org/about-us/

16. P McHenry, M Waters, F Hill, and S Lynch, AI Innovation Explored: Insights into AI Applications in Financial Services and Housing, House Committee on Financial Services, 18 July 2024. https://democrats-financialservices.house.gov/uploadedfiles/07.18.2024__ai_report_final.pdf

17. K Saleh, CFPB's Fair Lending Report: A Call to Action for Less Discriminatory Alternatives, Fairplay, n.d. https://fairplay.ai/cfpbs-fair-lending-report-a-call-to-action-for-less-discriminatory-alternatives/

18. Introducing SAM 2: The next generation of Meta Segment Anything Model for videos and images, Meta, 29 July 2024. https://ai.meta.com/blog/segment-anything-2/

7

Future of Work

Are we destined to repeat mistakes from the past?

By now, we can be certain that AI advancement will change the way we work and earn a living. While there are no lack of reports touting the potential of AI to create new opportunities and new ways of living/working (remember the one about how you can work less days/week), not enough attention has been paid by the regular media with respect to the negative impacts on marginalized communities—and the urgency we must take to change course.

Research conducted by the International Monetary Fund (IMF) predicted that AI could endanger 33% of jobs in advanced economies, 24% in emerging economies, and 18% in low-income countries. And since many of the countries in emerging and low-income economies tend to have less skilled workforces and infrastructure that can adopt AI and harness its full potential, they will likely benefit less from the technology, leading to increased inequality amongst the countries.[1] In the AI-enabled future, those who can't leverage AI will fall behind. Overall, IMF estimated that AI would affect almost 40% of jobs around the world, replacing some and complementing others. That echoed a report from Goldman Sachs in 2023, which estimated AI could replace the equivalent of 300 mn full-time jobs while creating others and boosting productivity.

Are we destined to repeat mistakes of the past—and risk widening the existing economic and opportunity gaps even more? How we best prepare and collaborate?

© The Author(s), under exclusive license to Springer Nature
Switzerland AG 2025
T. Lau, *Banking on (Artificial) Intelligence*, https://doi.org/10.1007/978-3-031-81647-5_7

In this chapter, we will review the jobs that are most likely to be impacted in finance and explore ideas that can help us rethink the future of work and education. We must be more intentional in creating opportunities for upskilling and reskilling, especially for those from underrepresented communities. Through investment in education and training for jobs of the future, we can help promote digital and AI literacy for a wider workforce to close the skills gap and build confidence and trust in AI (Fig. 7.1).

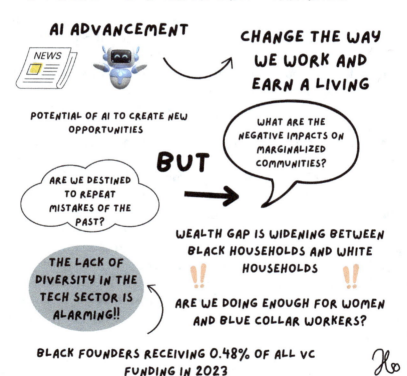

Fig. 7.1 Future of work

Education in the Age of AI

What will be the role of AI when it comes to education? Should teachers allow the use of generative AI tools in the classroom, or should they be banned?

This is a tough question to ask. On one hand, I think it is crucial that we teach children how to think, problem solve, and act creatively, such as writing an essay, without relying on tools such as ChatGPT to conduct the research and do the writing for them—which is a far easier way out. On the other hand, knowing how resourceful children can be, can we truly stop them from using the tools even if we try? And if not, would the time and effort be better spent showing them how to use the tools responsibly, and finding way to incorporate them into the curriculum?

As with all emerging technologies, however, this needs to be done thoughtfully. Take AI writing detectors for example. While many of these tools claim high accuracy rates, none of them are perfect. The emotional toll on a student wrongly accused of cheating can be high. More concerning is how these tools may be biased based on the students' writing style, particularly those that speak English as a second language. According to a Stanford University study on essays written by eighth grade students, several popular GPT detectors consistently misclassify non-native English writing samples as AI-generated, whereas those written by native English speakers are accurately identified.[2] According to the paper, the observed bias is likely due to the difference in writing styles: Non-native English writers tend to produce lower perplexity text compared to native authors, leading the AI detectors to misclassify the former group's writing as AI-generated text.

Although one might compare using AI tools to relying on calculators instead of doing manual computation, there is a difference in the level and type of work that generative AI tools are doing today. They are not merely automating the work—they are also replacing part of creativity that humans possess and changing the way we think and perform research.

While the jury may still be out on how generative AI can be effectively leveraged in educational settings, Hong Kong University of Science and Technology (HKUST) is testing the use of "AI lecturers". In Professor Pan Hui's "Social Media for Creatives" course, AI-generated instructors are assigned to teach a portion of the class, which is aimed for postgraduate students on immersive technologies and the impact of digital platforms.[3]

Will avatars of different styles, features, and accents impact how students learn, and to what extent will they be able to trust and connect with their AI lecturers?

Think Differently, Teach Differently

This reminds me of HKUST's efforts in encouraging students to explore and leverage the metaverse to bridge the physical distance between campuses, which I have covered in my previous book, The Metaverse Economy. The use of generative AI in classrooms is still new, and it will take time for us to fully understand how the technology will impact how students learn and collaborate. But I am encouraged by the passion and energy to explore the use of new technologies in our classrooms. The world is rapidly changing around us. How else do we prepare the leaders and innovators of tomorrow, than to navigate the new frontiers with them together in a safe environment? Trying by doing—isn't that what should encourage students to do?

As I write this chapter, I reflect upon my own education and upbringing. I went to school in a traditional all girls' Catholic school for twelve years. The curriculum back then offered two distinct paths starting at 10th Grade: Science or the arts. I chose the former, where I focused heavily on physics, chemistry, biology, and mathematics (including calculus and pure mathematics). My friends who chose the arts curriculum focused on history, geography, and literature. After high school, I enrolled in the Chemical Engineering degree at Rensselaer Polytechnic Institute in upstate New York, where the curriculum was once again very heavy STEM-focused.

To this date, I still joke that my brain operates like a flow chart. When I write in long form, I structure my thinking in boxes. And my first two books were formed in stacks of sticky notes. Often, I do wonder how different my career path would have been if I had made a different decision in high school or in college. What might I be doing now? And how would I fit in this new future of work? And how will the younger generation fare when the entry level jobs are automated? Is there a different way for them to learn?

In the past few years through my kids' education, I've come across a concept called adaptive learning. It is an educational method that uses AI to orchestrate the learning experience with the student, and present different resources to the student dynamically based on the answers that they provide. This makes the learning experience more effective and engaging. For example, ALEKS is an AI learning and assessment system that leverages Knowledge Space Theory to determine each student's knowledge of a particular subject (such as Algebra 1) and what they are ready to learn next. The solution was developed at the University of California and supported by funding from National Science Foundation, with courses available for grades 3–12 and higher education. For the consumer market, Duolingo, a popular language learning app, uses AI to analyze how users interact with the application and adapt the lessons and exercises according to the users' areas of strength and weakness.

As technology continues to advance, I see more opportunities for new ways of learning and teaching, such as through adaptive learning, to provide more engaging and effective learning environments for a wider group of students.

What can be Automated, will be Automated

Given what we know, can we future proof the kids' education and our career in an ever-changing world? How can we best get ready and adapt?

Take coding as an example. In Chapter 2, we have described the astounding efficiency gains by Amazon's generative AI assistant, Amazon Q, in upgrading their production Java systems. AI coding assistants that are meant to reduce repetitive tasks for programmers and improve their productivity can now close the experience gaps between entry-level developers and the more senior ones, essentially rendering the junior roles unnecessary. While the AI assistant might not be perfect (yet), they have drastically transformed how software development is being done. Beyond saving keystrokes by suggesting code, AI can also be used to translate code from one language to another. I do foresee challenges in the future though: If we become too reliant on AI to write the code, will we get to a point where we cannot understand the code enough to fix the bugs?

As always, there is nuance in the details, as not all developers may benefit the same from generative AI coding tools. In fact, according to a recent study conducted across Microsoft, Accenture, and an anonymous Fortune 100 company, while the usage of GitHub Copilot, an AI-based coding assistant, increases software developer productivity by 26%, the tool significantly raises task completion for more junior and recent hires, but not for developers who are more senior and with a longer tenure.[4]

When it comes to system development, writing lines of code is just one part of the tasks. We still need to design the system and have a holistic picture of what you are trying to build and why. We still need to understand the outcomes relative to the problems that need to be solved, and account for the risks when things could go wrong. In that regard and more, I remain hopeful that we will still need humans.

When I walked through the concept of this chapter with my friend, Diana Wu David, Author and Futurist at The Future Proof Lab, she shared some unique insights in the world of education that I had not thought of. What if students can have more opportunities to reflect on the nature of knowledge, think critically, and be more aware of how it is applied in real world scenarios? When education is approached from a more interdisciplinary manner, will this help us form a deeper understanding of how things are interconnected? Will we be more willing to embrace the concept of shared value?

While much is uncertain, I hope this will prepare our next generation to be more thoughtful in this increasingly uncertain and complex future world.

Skills of the Future

According to the World Economic Forum (WEF), 23% of global jobs will change in the next five years.[5] Unsurprisingly, AI and machine learning specialists, along with business intelligence analysts, information security analysts, fintech engineers, and data analysts and scientists are all on the top of the list for percentage of projected job creation; bank tellers rank the top in terms of percentage of potential jobs displaced. The increase in demand for data and AI-related specialists is in line with the robust increase in adoption of AI and machine learning across industries, and in particular, financial services, supply chain, and retail, which will in turn drive further transformation in operations and skills as organizations adapt.

If the world is changing, what are the essential skills that we will need to succeed, you may ask?

While it might be tempting to think that it's all about STEM skills, the truth may surprise you. As we discussed earlier in the chapter around the need to be well-rounded thinkers, the skillsets that organizations considered to be of growing importance focus on cognitive, interpersonal, and self-leadership, in addition to digital skills. According to McKinsey, some of these skills include critical thinking, communication, adaptability, self-motivation, empathy, teamwork, digital literacy, data literacy, and ethics.[6] This is not surprising; while AI can reduce the amount of time it takes us to complete certain tasks while automating and transforming other job functions, there is still plenty of work that needs to be done that will require human creativity and critical thinking. Simply knowing how to code is no longer enough. With technology underpinning everything that we do, those who know how to integrate new technologies in our environment and develop new ways of thinking and doing things will have the competitive edge. It is not just about increasing efficiency but developing new approaches and fostering innovation. To not only adapt but thrive, we need constant reinvention—a mindset that is crucial not just professionally but also personally and socially.

Being a self-learner has always been an important but undervalued skill. With the additional healthy living years that we have gained in the past few decades, coupled with changing nature of work where we are staying employed longer with more flexible ways of contributing, it is more crucial than ever that we continue to find ways to retool and learn new skills. After all, with the world changing around us, we cannot assume that what we have learned in early years will still be applicable after a few decades.

Luckily, there are now more learning platforms than ever that allow those with different skill sets and backgrounds to update their knowledge and expand their network. The topics range from technical skills such as programming and cybersecurity to management and people skills. While some are formal credential systems, there are many others that offer a la carte lessons and certificates, instructor-led or self-paced, which provide more flexibility to suit different needs of different learners. Such vast skill development opportunities also allow employers to focus more of the hiring on skills, rather than solely based on qualifications, and enable different pathways for employee advancement and role changes— another way to address the talent shortage that organizations face.

Before I started writing this book, I took a certificate class with Oxford University on artificial intelligence. I was pleasantly surprised by the diversity of people who attended, both geographically and professionally. But my best reward has been the community that remains; we have since formed an online group where we share ideas and organize in-person meetups.

It is time we reframe education and how learning is delivered. We must begin to integrate real-world application of skills in the curriculum and build stronger relationships with corporates—to make education more real and to improve the job prospects of the graduates. We need to recognize that there is simply no one-size-fits-all all approach when it comes to education. And learning is not a one-and-done exercise—it's something that needs to be refreshed when needs arise.

As the saying goes, talent is everywhere, opportunities are not. In a world that is quickly evolving and with increased digital connectivity, finding different pathways to connect people from different corners of the world to learn and collaborate will go a long way in bridging ecosystems and closing the talent and economic gaps. Navigating this change will require commitment and intentional effort from the industry as well as the government, to ensure that we are investing in the right places for success.

Some of my favorite examples come from partnerships, such as those between businesses and education institutions. Google.org, for instance, has allocated $25 million in funding to five education organizations, with the goal of helping educators and students access the skills and resources needed to thrive in the AI economy.[7] This includes collaboration with International Society for Technology in Education (ISTE), 4-H, and CodePath—which focuses on providing the education and career support for Black, Latino, Indigenous, and low-income students.

Another interesting initiative is the New York Jobs CEO Council, a coalition of CEOs who have committed to hiring 100,000 low-income New Yorkers by 2030, including 25,000 graduates from the City University of New York.[8] JPMorgan Chase, for instance, in collaboration with the New York Jobs CEO Council, offers apprenticeship where CUNY students who pursue an Applied Science degree in business management with specialization in finance and banking can earn eight college credits for their on-the-job training.

In fact, apprenticeship is another great way to address the talent shortage by helping students develop practical skills through blended on-the-job experience with classroom training or online courses, especially when traditional four-year college tuition may not be affordable or suitable for everyone. And this can serve as an on-ramp for new career pathways for youth and adults, and help workers reskill and upskill to meet the needs of the growing economy. The National Apprenticeship Act of 2023, for example, can create one million new apprenticeships, expand access to these opportunities for a more diverse group of workers into new and in-demand industry sectors and jobs.[9]

Programs such as the New York Jobs CEO Council and apprenticeships are crucial in closing the economic divide and providing opportunities for more people to become part of the economy of the future. The wealth gap between Black households and white households has widened since 1980 in the US, where the median white household now has $285,000 in wealth, compared to $45,000 for the median Black household. The playing field is hardly level and without intentional effort to change course, the divide will continue to grow.

The lack of diversity in the tech sector is also alarming, with Black founders receiving 0.48% of all VC funding in 2023. Black women are even more severely underrepresented—a trend that has persisted for years. As we continue our march toward an AI-enabled future, our current digital divide, as well as the disparity in access to resources, talent, and education, risk deepening the existing inequalities experienced by the underrepresented communities and exacerbating the gap between the have and the have-nots.

From job loss due to automation to multigenerational wealth disparity and racial bias, more needs to be done—and must be done.

Spotlight on Georgia Fintech Academy

The Georgia Fintech Academy is a talent development initiative supporting the University System of Georgia, which includes 26 public universities. Headquartered in Atlanta, a global fintech hub with over 260 fintech companies, the Academy plays a pivotal role in bridging the gap between academia and industry. By offering a comprehensive range of fintech courses that support both undergraduate and graduate degree programs, the Academy prepares students for dynamic careers in this rapidly evolving sector. Its curriculum is complemented by robust experiential learning opportunities made possible through strategic partnerships with leading industry players such as FIS, Visa, US Bank/Elavon, Global Payments, and Deluxe.

Since its inception, the Academy has engaged over 8000 students, with more than 2700 successfully transitioning into full-time fintech roles—demonstrating its effectiveness in workforce development. The Academy's holistic approach includes a speaker series, career fairs, hackathons, and a co-hosted student podcast, providing students with unparalleled access to practical insights, real-world experience, and valuable networking opportunities. These initiatives prepare students to excel in key areas such as payments, banking, artificial intelligence, machine learning, blockchain, and cybersecurity, positioning them at the forefront of the fintech industry.

"The future of fintech will be shaped by digital innovation and AI, and our mission at the Georgia Fintech Academy is to ensure that no one is left behind. By providing students with the skills, experiences, and industry connections they need, we are equipping the next generation to lead in a rapidly evolving world," commented Laura Gibson-Lamothe, Executive Director, Georgia Fintech Academy. "The key to success lies in bridging the gap between education and real-world application, preparing students to not only adapt but to thrive in the digital and AI-driven future."

As use cases for AI and generative AI evolve within the industry, it is essential that we stay in lockstep, continuously integrating these developments and learnings into the classroom to ensure our students are equipped with the most current and relevant knowledge.

Reskilling and Upskilling

If jobs around AI and data are going to increasingly dominate the future needs, do we have enough people to fill those roles?

The short answer is without intentional effort to reskill and upskill existing workers, it is unlikely. In fact, skill gaps and talent shortage are going to become increasingly one of the key constraints that will slow down our pace of innovation and development. And it is not difficult to understand why. As explained in Chapter 4, the private sectors, public institutions, and academia are all competing for the same talent, not just within borders but globally. And we have seen the extent at which big technology companies are willing to go, to secure the right talent back to the company. The fierce competition is precisely why developing existing workforce will take on renewed urgency as the competition for talent accelerates. The fear of hidden talent shortage is reflected in the 2024 Work Trend Index Annual Report released by LinkedIn and Microsoft, which shows that 55% of leaders are concerned about not having enough talent to fill the roles ahead.[10] And the share of professionals who are worried about their job being replaced by AI is the same as those who are quitting and looking for new jobs.

The talent gap is also echoed in a cross-industry study conducted by IBM, where CEOs surveyed indicated that 35% of their workforce will require upskilling and retraining in the next three years, compared to 6% in 2021. And to highlight how quickly technology is influencing the workplace, half of the CEOs said that they are hiring for roles that did not exist last year due to the rise of generative AI, while they are still struggling to fill key technology roles.[11]

So far, we have talked about education in the age of AI, what skillsets will be needed, and how learning needs to be reframed. But we have yet to address the elephant in the room. How will workers have access to opportunities to learn and become part of the digital economy? And whose responsibility is it to help workers adapt and upskill and how do they get ready?

In general, organizations that are AI mature are more likely to invest in upskilling and AI literacy programs, to retain the staff and also to ensure their employees can benefit from the technology—so that they can be more effective in what they do. For example, JPMorgan Chase has announced that they will provide prompt engineering training for all new hires, as the bank believes that AI is going to have a significant impact for their 60,000 developers and 80,000 operations and call-center employee.[12]

For self-learners, taking advantage of the various online learning platform is another great way to start, especially since many of the courses are free and there is a wide variety of subjects to choose from. In addition, organizations should also be intentional in creating career pathways that enable upward mobility—ability to learn and develop new skills can be a crucial differentiator especially when companies are facing workforce shortage.

And there is power of collaboration within the private sector in addressing the need to upskill talent, as in the case of the consortium formed in April

2024 and led by Accenture, Cisco, Eightfold, Google, IBM, Indeed, Intel, Microsoft, and SAP.[13] The AI-Enabled ICT Workforce Consortium has established a set of goals to develop and train 95 million people worldwide over the next decade, including AI, cybersecurity, and digital skills. For example, Cisco has committed to train 25 million people with cybersecurity and digital skills by 2032. IBM will skill 30 million people in digital skills, including 2 million in AI, by 2030. Intel is planning to collaborate with 30 countries to empower 30,000 institutions and train 30 million people with AI skills for current and future jobs by 2030. Microsoft will train and certify 10 million people from underserved communities with in-demand digital skills by 2025, and SAP will upskill 2 million people by the same time. Meanwhile, Google has allocated EUR 25 million in funding to support AI training and skills for people in European countries, as part of the AI Opportunity Initiative for Europe, with focus on vulnerable and underserved communities.[14] Separately in the US, Google.org has earmarked $75 million for an AI Opportunity Fund to help one million Americans learn essential AI skills, through funding for workforce development and education organizations.[15]

As I often say, intention drives outcome. I am hopeful that with proactive efforts and collaboration between the right stakeholders at the table, we can collectively do more to reskill and upskill the workforce, and foster new opportunities for more people, especially those who have been historically underrepresented. If our future is AI-led, we must ensure that everyone can be part of and benefit from this new economy. A rising tide lifts all boats—this is the perfect opportunity for us to catalyze change and create shared value for our society.

Who will be Impacted Most?

As AI use cases move from proof of concept to production, the question of "who will AI impact" becomes more real.

Many people have talked about how the current wave of automation would be different than previous cycles, where white-collar workers who previously were unaffected by prior workplace revolution will be impacted, especially when AI use cases move away from mundane tasks that can be easily automated to non-routine, cognitive tasks that are traditionally undertaken by those with higher education.

However, given that highly educated white-collar workers will also be the demographics group with more access to productivity enhancing AI tools compared to some of the lower-wage workers, along with exposure to more reskilling and upskilling opportunities, they might fare better than the those with less access to AI-related work opportunities.

What about older workers then? Will their tenure offer more protection compared to those who are entry level with less experience? Or will the negative bias—perceived notions that they are reluctant to learn and adapt new technologies—cost them their jobs?

And what about women? According to the United Nations, women's potential exposure to automation is much higher due to their over-representation in clerical occupations, sometimes more than double.[16] While this doesn't mean that women are twice as likely to lose their jobs due to automation compared to men, they are at much higher risk.

Some studies have also suggested that substantial AI gender gap as much as 25% is present in nearly all regions from high-income countries to low- and middle-income ones, and across sectors and occupations, suggesting that their likelihood to realize productivity gains from the technology will be less.[17] With AI's potential to drive a country's economic growth as well as workers' earning power, the ramifications from such disparity are vast. Beyond lost wages and productivity, we risk heading into a future world where women's voices are not heard, and we will be missing out on the ideas and innovation from half of the population.

For AI to achieve its full potential, policymakers must address the nuances that exist with different socio-demographic groups and provide targeted intervention to enable innovation to flourish in our society without deepening the inequalities that exist.

Is There Such Thing as an AI-Proof Job?

One of the things that I get asked quite often: Is there such thing as an AI-proof job?

It is an intriguing one, especially since AI will disrupt virtually everything that we do. Is there anywhere that may be considered safe?

While I don't have a crystal ball, in an AI-led future, the fastest growing roles will be those driven by technology and digital transformation. So, I think we can probably safely assume that the jobs that focus on helping organizations become data and AI-ready will likely be more secure than others. With that said, what are some key characteristics?

- Making data easy to use: This one is a no-brainer. Data is the lifeblood for AI—roles that can bring data together and make it easier for algorithms to leverage will have the key to the AI kingdom. This includes creating the standards and tools, as well as identifying the data needed for different use cases.

- Making data easy to track and share: Making the data easy to use is a great first step; being able to share the data, track where it is being used and how it is being used will be crucial.
- Making sense with data: To create value with data is where the magic happens—beyond driving operational efficiencies. How may we train our models with our own proprietary data sets? And how do we best integrate our data and technologies to create the capabilities that we need?

While it may be impossible to have a truly AI-proof job, we can stay resilient by upskilling and reskilling. After all, it is estimated that 44% of workers' skills will be disrupted in the next few years; we need to learn and adapt so that we can thrive in a changing environment.[18]

We simply cannot (and should not) compete with machines for speed. For starters, humans need to take breaks where algorithms can run 24 × 7. Instead, focus on areas where we excel—with analytical thinking and cognitive skills. Find roles where we can use AI to complement what we do best. Think about supply chain and AI's role for instance. Imagine when manual processes become digitalized, and organizations have greater access to data and visibility over the entire supply chain. The supply chain professionals can then leverage advanced technologies to get intelligent insights to optimize transportation plans and other logistics, they can also perform better demand forecasting, proactively anticipate and manage external risks (e.g. material shortages and extreme weather events), and improve cash flow management. Not only can we gain operational efficiencies (by doing things more efficiently with the help of various tools and automation), but we are also able to create more value in the process.

A Boost or the Boot?

As much as we keep telling everyone to not be afraid of AI, the narrative doesn't always fit the bill. News of companies displacing workers often make sensational headlines especially when increasing cost efficiencies is a popular topic for Wall Street during uncertain times. There is also a darker and more cynical side of AI when it comes to surveillance in the workplace. From tracking what people do on their work laptops or when they log in, to analyzing the tone of their voice when they are speaking to customers, companies are increasingly using technology to monitor and evaluate employees' performance. Will AI someday be used to help decide whether someone should be promoted or fired? The irony is this is not too far from science fiction; it reminds me of the episode "Nosedive" in the series Black Mirror, depicting a future where every interaction is rated and the ratings in turn determine one's socioeconomic status—from where you work to where you live.

As a recurring theme throughout the book, however, there are always two sides to the AI story. On one hand, we have learned that AI coding assistants tend to benefit entry-level employees more than those who are more experience, helping them get up-to-speed and perform their work faster. On the other hand, the efficiency gains most likely mean that we will need less entry-level positions, resulting in less employment opportunities with the junior staff. While organizations like to tout such productivity gains as a net positive where unfulfilling and mundane daily work is being automated by technology (such as simple code writing), leaving workers free to do more interesting and challenging tasks, somehow it just felt too easy to be true.

Klarna's bet on AI is a good illustration on the dualities of the technology. The CEO of the Swedish fintech famously said that their AI chatbot can do the equivalent work of 700 full time customer service agents.[19] Not only can it handle two-thirds of chat inquiries, but it also helps to reduce repeat inquiries from customers by 25%. Beyond the chatbot, Klarna has also seen tremendous productivity improvement fostered by AI applications in marketing and customer service. Unfortunately, the company is also planning to reduce headcount by as many as 2000. Can this be attributed solely to efficiency gain?[20]

Of course, there is more to AI and future of work than direct job displacement—it can also be about doing things differently. Ted Pick, CEO of Morgan Stanley, indicated that the use of AI has saved financial advisors between 10 and 15 hours a week for the bank, by way of advisors using the tool to transcribe client meeting notes, and fine-tune topics to discuss with their clients.[21] Banks can also leverage AI to re-imagine their business processes, for small business loans, for example.

AI can also be used for tax audits and can spell trouble for those who try to evade taxes. The IRS, for instance, reported that the agency was able to recover a record $1.3 billion in overdue taxes through audits, in addition to more than $375 million by cracking down on check fraud—all with the help of machine learning and fraud detection.[22] The use of technology to cross-check data and scan through documents to identify trends and anomalies is particularly useful here, as the agency receives about four billion forms each year. It is simply impossible for humans to efficiently and accurately go through such a massive volume of structured and unstructured data manually for enforcement. With the help of AI, not only can the agency recover a great amount of tax revenue, but the employees can now have more time to focus on improving the citizen services and drive more positive experiences.

While the jury is still out, one thing is for certain: Being adaptable and staying curious will be key to survival in the AI-led world.

Notes

1. G Melina, Mapping the World's Readiness for Artificial Intelligence Shows Prospects Diverge, IMF, 25 June 2024, https://www.imf.org/en/Blogs/Articles/2024/06/25/mapping-the-worlds-readiness-for-artificial-intelligence-shows-prospects-diverge
2. W Liang, M Yuksekgonul, Y Mao, E Wu, and J Zou, GPT detectors are biased against non-native English writers, Stanford University, 10 July 2023. https://arxiv.org/pdf/2304.02819
3. HKUST Introduces Asia's First "AI Lecturers" in Class to Promote Teaching Innovation, The Hong Kong University of Science and Technology, 8 March 2024. https://hkust.edu.hk/news/research-and-innovation/hkust-introduces-asias-first-ai-lecturers-class-promote-teaching
4. Z Cui, M Demirer, S Jaffe, L Musolff, S Peng, and T Salz, The Effects of Generative AI on High Skilled Work: Evidence from Three Field Experiments with Software Developers, SSRN, 3 September 2024. https://papers.ssrn.com/sol3/papers.cfm?abstract_id=4945566&utm_source=substack&utm_medium=email
5. The Future of Jobs Report 2023, World Economic Forum, 30 April 2023. https://www.weforum.org/publications/the-future-of-jobs-report-2023/
6. The skills revolution and the future of learning and earning, World government summit 2023 and McKinsey & Company, n.d. https://www.mckinsey.com/~/media/mckinsey/industries/education/our%20insights/the%20skills%20revolution%20and%20the%20future%20of%20learning%20and%20earning/the-skills-revolution-and-the-future-of-learning-and-earning-report-f.pdf

7. M Johnson, Google.org announces new AI funding for students and educators, Google.org, 18 September 2024. https://blog.google/out reach-initiatives/google-org/google-ai-initiatives-funding-educators-students/
8. New York Jobs CEO Council. https://nyjobsceocouncil.org/
9. Labor Leaders Introduce Bipartisan Bill to Expand Apprenticeships, Congressman Bobby Scott, 25 April 2023. https://bobbyscott.house. gov/media-center/press-releases/labor-leaders-introduce-bipartisan-bill-expand-apprenticeships
10. AI at Work Is Here. Now Comes the Hard Part, Microsoft, 8 May 2024. https://www.microsoft.com/en-us/worklab/work-trend-index/ai-at-work-is-here-now-comes-the-hard-part
11. CEO Study: 6 hard truths CEOs must face, IBM Institute for Business Value, 5 June 2024. https://www.ibm.com/downloads/cas/QJ2 BYLZG
12. H Levitt, JPMorgan Says Every New Hire Will Get Training for AI, Bloomberg, 20 May 2024. https://www.bloomberg.com/news/articles/ 2024-05-20/jpmorgan-s-erdoes-says-every-new-hire-will-get-training-for-ai?srnd=technology-vp
13. Leading Companies Launch Consortium to Address AI's Impact on the Technology Workforce, Cisco, 4 April 2024. https://www.prnews wire.com/news-releases/leading-companies-launch-consortium-to-add ress-ais-impact-on-the-technology-workforce-302107835.html
14. M Brittin, Launching the AI Opportunity Initiative for Europe, Google, 12 February 2024. https://blog.google/around-the-globe/goo gle-europe/google-ai-opportunity-initiative-europe/
15. Google.org's $75 M AI Opportunity Fund for the United States, Google Public Policy, 26 April 2024. https://publicpolicy.google/art icle/AI-opportunity-fund/
16. Mind the AI Divide, United Nations—Office of the Secretary-General's Envoy on Technology, 2024. https://www.un.org/techenvoy/ sites/www.un.org.techenvoy/files/MindtheAIDivide.pdf
17. N Otis, K Cranney, S Delecourt, and R Koning, Global Evidence on Gender Gaps and Generative AI, Center for Open Science, 2024. https://ideas.repec.org/p/osf/osfxxx/h6a7c.html
18. The Future of Jobs Report 2023, World Economic Forum, April 30 2023. https://www.weforum.org/publications/the-future-of-jobs-report-2023/digest/
19. M Cerullo, Klarna CEO says AI can do the job of 700 workers. But job replacement isn't the biggest issue. CBS News,

5 March 2024. https://www.cbsnews.com/news/klarna-ceo-ai-chatbot-replacing-workers-sebastian-siemiatkowski/

20. T Gerken, Klarna: AI lets us cut thousands of jobs—but pay more, BBC, 28 August 2024. https://www.bbc.com/news/articles/c80e1g p9m9zo

21. N Nishant and T Bautzer, Morgan Stanley CEO says AI could save financial advisers 10–15 hours a week, Reuters, 10 June 2024. https://www.reuters.com/technology/morgan-stanley-ceo-says-ai-could-save-financial-advisers-10-15-hours-week-2024-06-10/

22. K Hube, The IRS Will Use AI to Do More Tax Audits. What You Need to Know. Barron's, 12 October 2024. https://www.barrons.com/articles/stock-market-economy-germany-5492d7b7

8

Win at all Costs?

Can purpose, profits, and responsibility find harmony in an AI-led world?

Sustaining AI model training and inference requires a large amount of energy as well as water—to support onsite server cooling and offsite electricity generation. It is estimated that we would need as much as 4.2–6.6 billion cubic meters of water withdrawal by 2027, which is more than the total annual water withdrawal from 4 to 6 Denmark or half of UK.

How does AI intersect with sustainability? How do resource-hungry AI models contribute to an organization's carbon footprint? Technology innovation cannot come at the expense of our planet. As we journey toward a new era, we must consider the environmental impact of our actions and ensure that we will still have a viable place to call home.

This chapter aims to bring our attention to the high toll on our environment due to AI development and operations, a topic that is less discussed in the age of AI abundance, and the role of financial services in fostering the transition to a more sustainable world (Fig. 8.1).

© The Author(s), under exclusive license to Springer Nature Switzerland AG 2025
T. Lau, *Banking on (Artificial) Intelligence*, https://doi.org/10.1007/978-3-031-81647-5_8

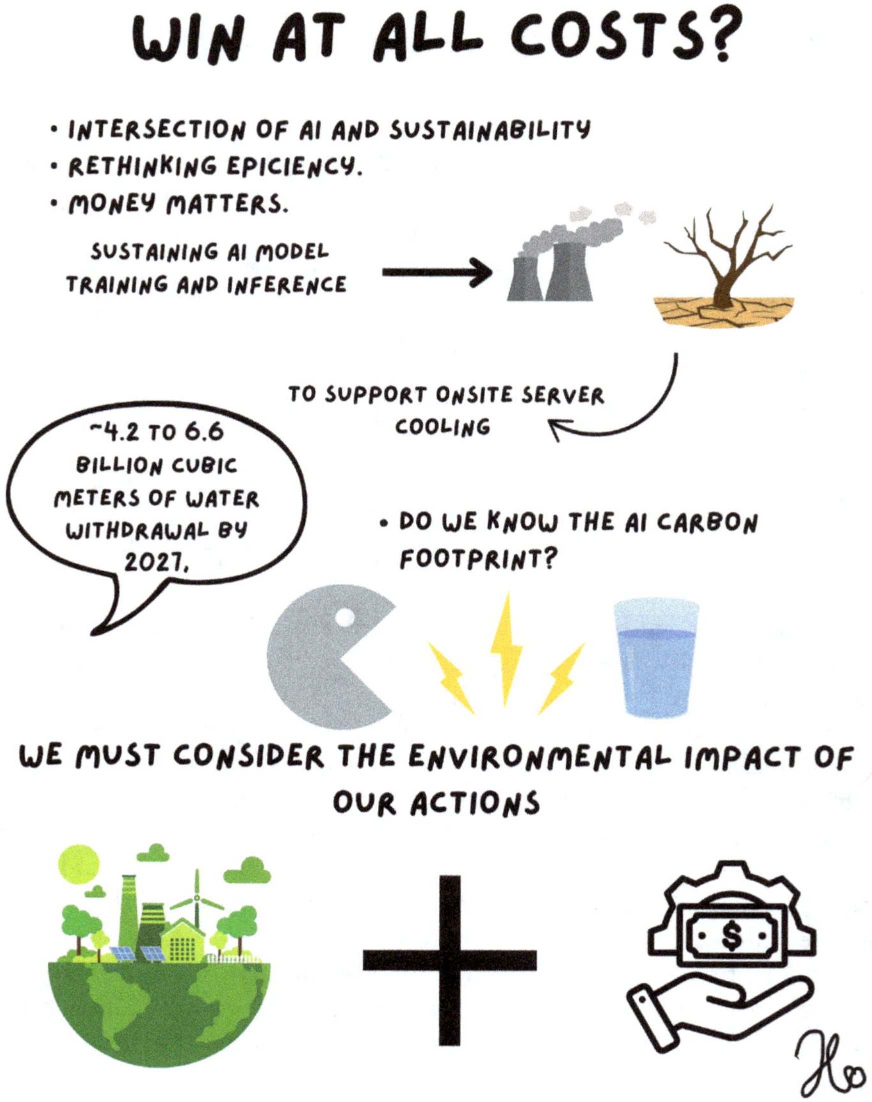

Fig. 8.1 Win at all costs?

Environmental Impact of AI

Artificial intelligence is undoubtedly having a transformative impact on many aspects of our lives, and we are just at the very tip of the iceberg as new use cases are discovered at a rapid pace. Beyond finding potential cure for untreatable diseases, AI can also help us create more efficient ways to produce and distribute energy, leading us to a more sustainable future. However, such advances also come at a cost. It is no secret that training large-language models can be resource-intensive; an immense amount of power is required to keep the servers running and stay cool. For example, according to MIT Technology Review, using generative AI to create an image can require as much energy as charging up a phone; generating 1000 images with Stable Diffusion XL will emit as much carbon dioxide as driving just over four miles in a gas-powered car.[1]

What is uncertain, however, is how that balances out the potential gains in efficiency and innovation. While that question will likely be left unanswered for a while, what is real and concerning is the existing impact on the environment, as evidenced by how some of the technology firms are pulling back from their original emission targets.

Era of Hyper-Consumption

The omnipresence of AI is impossible to ignore, especially in the past two years when development and adoption have gone on overdrive. AI Overview—a summary of information generated by AI, leveraging information across the internet and Google's Knowledge Graph—now appears on the top of the page when you perform a Google search on a topic. Personal AI assistants such as Google Gemini and Microsoft Copilot are embedded in the suite of productivity tools from email to worksheet and more.

The increase in usage is evident in the sustainability reports produced by some of the big technology companies. Some of the statistics made available underscore the importance and urgency of finding more energy efficient ways to operate. Take Google as an example, who reported that its greenhouse gas emissions increased by an astonishing 48% from 2019 to 2023.[2] This is hardly surprising, considering the popularity with generative AI applications such as OpenAI's ChatGPT, which is expected to more than double the global data center electricity consumption.[3] Google search could witness a staggering tenfold increase in electricity demand when it's fully implemented with AI. According to one estimate from the International Energy Agency (IEA), the AI industry is expected to consume at least ten times its demand in 2023.[4] It is important to note that IEA estimates include *all* data center activities: AI, streaming, electric vehicles, and other activities in our modern lives. With the exception of Google, most tech companies do not offer a specific breakdown by categories, and there is no agreed upon method to estimate environment impact of training AI models, so there is no way of knowing the exact energy consumption by AI.

Nevertheless, US electricity demand is forecasted to exceed supply within the next few years, with data centers making up the bulk of the increase. And while North America is the largest market for generative AI, the rest of the world is catching up with quickly. For example, with one of the lowest corporate tax rates in the EU, Ireland's data center sector is expected to grow by 65% in the next few years. As a result, they are forecasted to double their consumption of electricity from 2022 to 2026, representing 32% of the country's total electricity demand, assuming most of the approved projects can be connected to the system.[5]

Meanwhile, data center capacity in the Asia Pacific (APAC) is expected to more than double in the next five years to keep up with the demand in AI and cloud services, with the share of global revenue from the region estimated to increase from 14 to 20% by 2028, according to S&P Global.[6] Unfortunately, since many of these data centers are run by non-sustainable power sources such as fossil fuels, such rapid expansion in capacity and growing demand in the region will negatively impact the countries' net-zero targets. More clean energy is needed.

In addition to increased demand for electricity, water consumption will also increase, as clean water is needed to cool the servers. In my first book, Beyond Good, I wrote about the risks of Day Zero, the day when the public water supply runs out in a city or a region. Considering the growing water shortages in Asian regions including India, Nepal, Bangladesh, and China, expanding data center capacity will likely exacerbate the situation. Not to mention, the rise in electricity consumption will also expose the region to additional carbon emissions. Designing more sustainable and less energy-intensive data centers must be at the forefront of ecosystem development considerations. We also need to ensure the availability of reliable data, so that we can better identify the impact of innovation, understand future trends and plan for change appropriately.

All hope is not lost, however. In fact, the increased demand for electricity has acted as a catalyst to propel the search for cleaner energy and to get AI to become more efficient and do more with less energy.

Rethinking Efficiency

According to the IEA, total electricity consumption by the data centers could more than double between 2022 and 2026, reaching more than 1000 terawatt-hours by 2026, roughly equivalent to the electricity consumption of Japan.[7]

Given the drastic increase, a simple question ensued: When will our demand exceed the supply?

The answer might be closer than we think. While estimates tend to fluctuate, one study by Bain indicated that by 2028, utilities would need to increase energy generation by 7% and 26% above the 2023 total.[8] That is simply staggering—and it will take a balancing act to maneuver between pushing the boundaries to meet new demands versus sustaining existing needs in an affordable, sustainable, and reliable manner.

Virginia, for example, is home to the world's largest concentration of data centers. Northern Virginia, with its proximity to Washington D.C., is known as the data center alley, with the largest data center market in the US.[9] In one of the filings to the state, Dominion Energy, the largest utility company in the state of Virginia, reported that the data center industry in Virginia had a peak metered load of almost 2.8 GW in 2022—roughly 1.5 times the capacity of the company's North Anna nuclear facility.[10] As demand is projected to grow—advocacy groups are pushing the state to relook at how the state is planning to balance the needs of the data center industry, the transition to clean power, and the ability of the current grid to support the needs of the existing communities.

There are reasons why some governors may be more welcoming to the development of such digital infrastructure facilities in their states despite the opposition from advocacy groups, however. One of which is the lucrative tax revenue from the operations of the data centers. For each data center, purchases of hardware and software licenses, in addition to the ongoing maintenance, can generate substantial state and local tax revenue. In Northern Virginia for example, computer equipment purchases for data centers brought in $582 million in 2023 alone, 170% higher compared to 2021 and 2.5 times the tax revenue from car sales.[11] In Nebraska, the annual property taxes from a data center facility are estimated to be 110 times greater than those from agricultural land.[12]

Getting More with Less

Given electricity is one of the necessary ingredients—and a constraint—perhaps one of the most exciting developments of late is around energy efficiency: How can we get more output with less?

The NVIDIA Blackwell platform, for example, can enable organizations to build and run real-time generative AI on LLMs scaling up to 10 trillion parameters, at up to 25 times less cost and energy consumption, compared to their previous model.[13] Among the tech companies expected to adopt the new platform includes AWS, Dell, Google DeepMind, Meta, Microsoft, OpenAI, Oracle, Tesla, and xAI.

Beyond improving efficiency in the software stack, another option that the tech industry is actively pursuing is small language models (SLM). These models are smaller in size and trained using smaller amounts of data—which means they require less compute resources to operate. While these smaller models are not meant to substitute or replace the large language models, they can be complementary, and organizations can choose the right mix based on what the applications that they need to build and the resources available.

There are also other added benefits with SLMs as well. For example, SLMs can be embedded on device and operate at the edge, and users can use the AI capabilities on their mobile devices even if they do not have good connectivity. Since the SLMs can work offline, you don't need to be connected to the cloud every time you need to run it, as in the case with big models.

In fact, using the low-data and low-compute SLMs is an approach favored by the African AI Network, a collaborative effort that aims to connect 520 million speakers across the African continent to the global digital society.[14] And increasingly, this is also an approach being adopted by the AI communities in China as well, since smaller amounts of data require less resource to train—enabling developers to build applications that are trained on models that are competitive but yet, cost five to ten times less.[15]

Pursuit of Clean Energy Alternatives

To continue the current pace of transformation, some big tech players are not leaving anything to chance as the utilities industry look for new solutions. And increasingly, the tech industry is setting their sight on the clean energy market to help fuel their AI ambitions and to fulfill their commitment for a 24/7 carbon-free future. Beyond the typical solar, wind, and hydropower, there are some interesting developments being explored in nuclear and fusion power.

In a first of its kind deal, Google signed an agreement to purchase nuclear energy from seven small modular reactors (SMRs) to be built by startup Kairos Power.[16] The first unit will come online by 2030 with the rest through 2035, producing a total of 500 megawatts for the grid to power one AI data-center campus for Google (or a midsize city).[17] Currently, there are only three SMRs in the world; this new one will be the first one on US soil. And instead of using water to cool the nuclear reactor, molten fluoride salt will be used instead.

The Google – Kairos Power partnership is one of few in the tech industry. Earlier in the year, Amazon Web Services acquired a nuclear-powered data center campus from Talen Energy. Separately, Microsoft is working with Constellation Energy to restart Three Mile Island, the site of the partial nuclear meltdown in 1979.

But the more exciting story is around Helion Energy, a fusion research company based in Everett, Washington. In 2023, Microsoft announced a power purchase agreement with Helion to purchase electricity from Helion Energy's first fusion power plant, which is scheduled for deployment in 2028. This will mark the first time a fusion company is commercializing the process that powers the sun—a marvelous engineering achievement if they can pull it off. And this will also signify a cheaper and faster way of bringing more clean energy to the grid while meeting the dramatic increase in demand for electricity.

Interestingly, Helion counts Sam Altman as one of their financial backers, with the OpenAI CEO investing $375 million into the startup.[18] This makes sense, especially given the crucial role that energy plays in the future of AI; without radical innovation, we will soon face constraints from the existing power grid. As AI adoption grows, we need access to reliable, clean, and cheap energy source, to help meet the demands of electricity, lower the cost of training and running complex AI models, and meet net-zero goals. Affordable energy will offer more sustainable pathways to bring AI solutions to communities everywhere.

As the saying goes, sky is the limit.

Can We Make AI Less Thirsty?

Besides electricity, growth of the data center economy also puts an immense strain on water, which is used to cool the servers in the data centers. While it may be a less talked about topic and we don't have a set of standards and regulations to govern what needs to be reported, it is nevertheless an important topic given the increasing water scarcity that people face.

According to Washington Post, a 100-word email that is generated once a week by an AI chatbot using OpenAI's ChatGPT-4 uses approximately 519 ml of water.[19] The cumulative effect for one person after one year generating one 100-word email per week equates to about 27 liters—approximately 1.43 water cooler jugs. Although it may seem negligible, consider the fact that ChatGPT attracts more than 200 million weekly active users. Imagine 5400 liters of drinking water—or 286 million water cooler jugs.

Remember the earlier estimates that I cited with respect to increased energy consumption? According to a paper released in 2023, the amount of water withdrawn by data centers is expected to be between 4.2 billion to 6.6 billion cubic meters by 2027, which is more than the total annual water withdrawal of 4–6 Denmark, or half of the UK.[20]

Even though these are estimates, they are stark, especially given how severe water scarcity is around the world. Food systems are already running out of fresh water and cities are sinking with aquifers running dry. According to a report released by the Global Commission on the Economics of Water, nearly 3 billion people and more than half of the world's food production are in areas where the total water storage will likely decline.[21] Simply put, without intervention, half of our food system is in the brink of collapse due to water scarcity.

With the situation exacerbated by the impact of climate change and rapid adoption of AI, there is an urgent need for more transparency on water usage by the tech industry (data centers, in particular), a firm commitment to improving water use efficiency, as well as innovation to reducing dependency on freshwater supply for cooling and humidification needs. Some promising strides have been made for instance: 22% of Google's total data center water withdrawal in 2023 was reclaimed wastewater and other non-potable water.[22] We need more.

And we must also be mindful of where the data centers are located. In Microsoft's case, 42% of the big tech company's total water consumption comes from areas with water stress.[23] The impact of being able to operate these data centers in a more energy and water-efficient matter will be crucial to the survival of these regions and their communities. Santiago, Chile, for instance, is one of the largest data center hubs in Latin America, with 16 data centers having been approved in 12 years. However, the country is also experiencing substantial drought that is expected to last more than a decade till 2040. In September 2024, activists in the country successfully forced Google to change its original data center design to a new one using air-based cooling system instead of water cooling.[24]

We must find ways to measure and monitor the water footprint, for example, so that we can optimize where and when to train and deploy the AI models to get to the best model accuracy with the least water consumed.

The world has a water crisis and there is a cost to inaction. It is imperative that we double down on innovation and actively explore ways to protect freshwater resources around the world.[25] Access to clean water is a right, and innovation must not come at the expense of community needs and the well-being of our planet, especially given the increasing climate-related risks.

Rethink. Not Repeat

As we approach the end of the second section of the book, I'd like to take a short pause and look back at what we've discussed so far. The hype of AI is very much real and present with us. While AI is not a new technology, generative AI, thanks to OpenAI's ChatGPT, has brought the tech right at the doorstep of every user—inviting them to try and experience its simplicity and power. It is no wonder why so many people are mesmerized by it. The tools have enabled us to be in command of things that were unimaginable before. We can now expand our abilities and express our emotions and our thoughts through words, images, audio, and videos—with just a few clicks and prompts. Our workplace has gone through a drastic transformation as well with everything getting done much quicker—from coding to marketing and customer service.

And we are just at the very beginning of a journey—what some might call a revolution. AI assistants will soon take over the mundane tasks that no one wants to do, freeing up humans to sit back and find something more fulfilling to do. Choose your own adventure, so to speak. And AI will keep all of us healthy, happy, and connected. The list goes on.

But if that is the end game, how do we get there? What do we have to sacrifice to get to the state where AI can bring the prosperity that we are promised? And who can ultimately afford to play? For those who have been disenfranchised and left behind in the last digital revolution, does this new world include them? Or are they merely an afterthought?

Many of us have seen a version of this movie played out before. The internet was supposed to bridge the physical distance that separates us, bring us together and enable all of us to be part of the innovation ecosystem. But in the past few years, we have witnessed the public discourse and fragmentation of our society. We have seen governments competing for their own interests rather than collaborating to improve the well-being for more people. We have seen the dark side of technology and the toll on those who are voiceless and forgotten.

Do we believe that this time will be different?

This is a tough question to answer. Throughout my writing journey in preparing for this book, I have spoken to both the dreamers and the doers from around the world. I have talked to the optimists and the pessimists in technology and financial services. I came away with more questions than answers. But I also felt something else: A resolve to do something different— a drive to do it better this time around—in spite of the potential challenges that we may face, including political uncertainties.

While we may not all agree on the how, but we know we need to change— because what we have is not quite working the way we need it to. And AI is not just extracting from our society; it is creating value for us as well. And the financial services industry is at an interesting crossroads—acting both as a beneficiary of the technology and an enabler of it, via tech adoption and capital investment.

Sensing the economic opportunities for growth in the energy sector due to demands from accelerated computing and generative AI, BlackRock is planning a $30 billion AI investment fund with Microsoft to build data centers and energy projects, with NVIDIA joining to advise on factory design and integration, and MGX—an Abu Dhabi-backed investment firm—as general partner with Microsoft.[26]

With much of our systems written in COBOL, a programming language developed in 1959, incremental changes are no longer sufficient. To keep up with the needs of our modern-day economy, our core banking infrastructure is in dire need of modernization. And AI is the perfect tool to help us get there.

In the next section, we will explore the enablers that we will need to succeed in the AI-enabled world. We will look at the approaches undertaken by different regulatory bodies and discuss important values that are core to our shared future.

And we will end the book with hope; because there is still so much good in the world that we must fight for.

Notes

1. C Crownhart, AI is an energy hog. This is what it means for climate change. MIT Technology Review, 23 May 2024. https://www.tec hnologyreview.com/2024/05/23/1092777/ai-is-an-energy-hog-this-is-what-it-means-for-climate-change/
2. J Calma, Google's carbon footprint balloons in its Gemini AI era, The Verge, 2 July 2024. https://www.theverge.com/2024/7/2/24190874/ google-ai-climate-change-carbon-emissions-rise
3. Y Xue, Booming GenAI demand to propel doubling of Asia–Pacific data centre capacity by 2028, South China Morning Post, 28 July 2024. https://www.scmp.com/business/article/3272205/booming-genai-demand-propel-doubling-asia-pacific-data-centre-capacity-2028
4. Electricity 2024, International Enery Agency, May 2024. https://iea. blob.core.windows.net/assets/18f3ed24-4b26-4c83-a3d2-8a1be51c8 cc8/Electricity2024-Analysisandforecastto2026.pdf
5. Electricity 2024, International Energy Agency, May 2024. https://iea. blob.core.windows.net/assets/18f3ed24-4b26-4c83-a3d2-8a1be51c8 cc8/Electricity2024-Analysisandforecastto2026.pdf
6. Y Xue, Booming GenAI demand to propel doubling of Asia–Pacific data centre capacity by 2028, South China Morning Post, 28 July 2024. https://www.scmp.com/business/article/3272205/booming-genai-demand-propel-doubling-asia-pacific-data-centre-capacity-2028
7. Electricity 2024, International Energy Agency, May 2024. https:// www.iea.org/reports/electricity-2024/executive-summary
8. M Rouch, A Denman, P Hanburg, P Renno, and E Gray, Utilities Must Reinvent Themselves to Harness the AI-Driven Data Center Boom, Bain & Company, 10 October 2024. https://www.bain.com/ insights/utilities-must-reinvent-themselves-to-harness-the-ai-driven-data-center-boom/
9. P Taylor, Data centers in the U.S.—statistics & facts, Statista, 2 July 2024. https://www.statista.com/topics/10667/data-centers-in-the-us/# topicOverview
10. Virginia Electric and Power Company's 2023 Integrated Resource Plan.

filing pursuant to Va. Code, McGuireWoods LLP, 1 May 2023. https://cdn-dominionenergy-prd-001.azureedge.net/-/media/pdfs/glo bal/company/2023-va-integrated-resource-plan.pdf

11. Data Center Growth Has Economic Ripple Effects, CBRE, 23 May, 2024. https://www.cbre.com/insights/briefs/data-center-growth-has-economic-ripple-effects

12. Data Center Growth Has Economic Ripple Effects, CBRE, 23 May, 2024. https://www.cbre.com/insights/briefs/data-center-growth-has-economic-ripple-effects

13. NVIDIA Blackwell Platform Arrives to Power a New Era of Computing. NVIDIA, 18 March 2024. https://nvidianews.nvidia. com/news/nvidia-blackwell-platform-arrives-to-power-a-new-era-of-computing

14. Solve the African language problem for inclusive AI development, The UN agency for digital technologies, 6 June 2024. https://www.itu.int/ hub/2024/06/solve-the-african-language-problem-for-inclusive-ai-dev elopment/

15. E Olcott, Chinese AI groups get creative to drive down cost of models, Financial Times, 18 October 2024. https://www.ft.com/content/0a6 da1bb-2bda-40f3-9645-97877eb0947c

16. M Terrell, New nuclear clean energy agreement with Kairos Power, Google, 14 October 2024. https://blog.google/outreach-initiatives/sus tainability/google-kairos-power-nuclear-energy-agreement/

17. J Hiller, Google Backs New Nuclear Plants to Power AI, The Wall Street Journal, 14 October 2024. https://www.wsj.com/business/ene rgy-oil/google-nuclear-power-artificial-intelligence-87966624

18. J Temple, This startup says its first fusion plant is five years away. Experts doubt it. MIT Technology Review, 10 May 2023. https:// www.technologyreview.com/2023/05/10/1072812/this-startup-says-its-first-fusion-plant-is-five-years-away-experts-doubt-it/

19. P Verma and S Tan, A bottle of water per email: the hidden environmental costs of using AI chatbots, The Washington Post, 18 September 2024. https://www.washingtonpost.com/technology/2024/ 09/18/energy-ai-use-electricity-water-data-centers/

20. P Li, J Yang, M Islam, and S Ren, Making AI Less "Thirsty": Uncovering and Addressing the Secret Water Footprint of AI Models, Cornell University, 29 October 2023. arXiv:2304.03271v3.

21. The economics of water: Valuing the hydrological cycle as a global common good, Global Commission on the Economics of Water, 17 October 2024. https://economicsofwater.watercommission.org/report/ economics-of-water.pdf

22. Google Environmental Report, Google. n.d. https://www.gstatic.com/gumdrop/sustainability/google-2024-environmental-report.pdf

23. K Wiggers, Demand for AI is driving data center water consumption sky high, TechCrunch, 19 August 2024. https://techcrunch.com/2024/08/19/demand-for-ai-is-driving-data-center-water-consumption-sky-high/

24. M Sellman and A Vaughan, 'Thirsty' ChatGPT uses four times more water than previously thought, The Sunday Times, 4 October 2024. https://www.thetimes.com/uk/technology-uk/article/thirsty-chatgpt-uses-four-times-more-water-than-previously-thought-bc0pqswdr?region=global

25. 2024 Environmental Sustainability Report Data Fact Sheet, Microsoft, n.d. https://query.prod.cms.rt.microsoft.com/cms/api/am/binary/RW1lmju

26. B Masters, A Gara, J Fontanella-Khan, and S Morris, BlackRock and Microsoft plan $30bn fund to invest in AI infrastructure, Financial Times, 17 September 2024. https://www.ft.com/content/4441114b-a105-439c-949b-1e7f81517deb

9

Ownership, Rights, and Governance

Are we shaped by society, or do we shape it?

We have gone through the hype cycle. We have explored the reality and dived into the opportunities and challenges in implementing emerging technology solutions—with potential to benefit more of humankind. While we might have been living in the age of AI abundance, the time for governance has finally arrived. With regulators playing catch up, and regulatory bodies worldwide taking different approaches, what will the future be like? How can creators and consumers protect their rights and thrive in the digital economy?

In this chapter, we will explore the tug of war between big tech companies, creators, consumers, and news organizations on content ownership and rights. We will also review the state of regulations on AI around the world, including the AI Treaty, EU Artificial Intelligence Act, as well as the White House Executive Order on the Safe, Secure, and Trustworthy Development and Use of Artificial Intelligence (Fig. 9.1).

© The Author(s), under exclusive license to Springer Nature
Switzerland AG 2025
T. Lau, *Banking on (Artificial) Intelligence*, https://doi.org/10.1007/978-3-031-81647-5_9

Fig. 9.1 Ownership, rights, and governance

Whose Rights are we Protecting?

In the era of generative AI, where AI developers are crawling the internet for data to train their AI models, the question around content ownership and copyright has taken on a new level of urgency.

One of the issue stems from the data needed to train generative AI models. As we have discussed throughout this book, data is a critical input (or the lifeblood) for generative AI models, and these models are only as good as the datasets that they are trained on. Here, web crawlers are typically employed to pull massive amount of public data from the internet to be used as training data for the foundation models for OpenAI, Anthropic, and other AI companies. And therein lies the problem. Such data often includes news websites, academic forums, social media, individual blogs, personal websites, etc. In the vast universe of AI data, what can be used (and not used) for training and under what circumstances? For content creators, is there an effective means for them to opt out of AI training, and pursue legal action to protect their intellectual property? And for AI companies, as time goes on and data becomes more restricted, what will happen to their models, some of which require large pool of updated data?

In December 2023, The New York Times filed a lawsuit against OpenAI and Microsoft for copyright infringement by using the newspaper's articles to train the tech companies' AI chatbots without permission, making the paper the first major media outlet to sue OpenAI.[1] In countering the lawsuit, OpenAI and Microsoft challenged that using The Times' content to train their AI products is considered fair use. In October 2024, News Corp-owned Dow Jones and New York Post filed suit against Perplexity AI, alleging the company of copying the publishers' work into a database to provide answers to users' queries.[2] Right before this lawsuit was filed, New York Times has sent Perplexity a notice, demanding the startup to stop using its content without consent.

Interestingly, prior to the Dow Jones lawsuit against Perplexity for copyright infringement, news organizations have signed licensing agreements with OpenAI, allowing the startup to use their copyrighted materials for their generative AI chatbot in exchange for a fee. This includes OpenAI's partnership agreements with News Corp, Financial Times, Axel Springer, and the Associated Press to license their content.

In July 2024, US Senators Marsha Blackburn, Maria Cantwell, and Martin Heinrich, introduced the COPIED Act (Content Origin Protection and Integrity from Edited and Deepfaked Media Act), to fight the rise of harmful deepfakes and set guidelines for marking, authenticating, and detecting AI-generated content, and to protect journalists and artists (such as songwriters) from having their content being used without prior consent.[3] The Act would also direct the NIST to create standards and guidelines to prove the origin of content and detect synthetic content, and would make it illegal to remove digital watermarks.

Artists and creators are becoming increasingly aware of the need to come to a mutual agreement with the industries over the concerns of ownership and rights. Imagine a company using AI to learn the voice of an actress and create a replica of it—without prior consent and compensation, instead of hiring her for the job. Or imagine someone feeding a digital copy of this chapter that you are reading to an AI program, and have the AI mimic my style of writing to create a new book without my consent.

In March 2024, Lego posted a series of images related to the popular Ninjago theme, a superhero TV series produced by Lego Group. Unfortunately, the content was created using generative AI and went "outside of the process" according to Lego.[4] It was eventually taken down. As a tool, generative AI can help break barriers. For example, anyone in anywhere with an idea can now build something creative with the help of generative AI. However, since this 'new' design by generative AI is based on what the model has been trained on, i.e., previous work by other designers, can this new creative still be considered original? And who owns the intellectual property rights?

Without meaningful protections, creators and journalists are exposed. It is not surprisingly, therefore, that in recent months, we have seen Hollywood video game performers gone on strike and voiced their concerns.[5] Publishing and groups representing artists have applauded the introduction of the COPIED Act; though at the time of writing the article, it is uncertain when the bill will be passed if at all.

This also comes at a time when technology has made it easy and cost effective to create astonishingly accurate digital representations of people. I have tried a few of these software tools over the past few months, and I have presented my own deepfake video in various conferences. Most people who have seen it, especially those who have not met me prior to the presentation, were shocked at how real these videos seem. We have already seen how bad actors could use these tools to exploit unassuming victims for financial gains in prior chapters; as technology continues to mature, this will pose an increasingly dangerous threat to the public.

And the outcome of the lawsuits between the news organizations and AI companies—when they are settled—will have far reaching implications. How best can media companies protect their intellectual property within the boundaries of the current legal framework, and is that sufficient? At the same time, should tech companies re-evaluate their risk management strategies to address liabilities from potential legal challenges?

As adoption of AI continues and new use cases are created, one thing is clear: regulations are playing catchup, and jurisdictions around the world are taking different approaches.

In July 2023, the White House secured voluntary commitments from a group of tech and AI companies to advance safe, secure, and trustworthy AI development. These seven companies consisted of Microsoft, Amazon, Google, Meta, Anthropic, OpenAI, and Inflection. Two months later in September 2023, the administration secured a second round of voluntary commitments from eight additional tech companies, including Adobe, Cohere, IBM, NVIDIA, Palantir, Salesforce, Scale AI, and Stability.[6]

As we look back on the journey from the issuance of the White House Executive Order in October 2023, there are a few wins that are worth mentioning, including[7]:

- Secured commitment for companies to conduct red-teaming exercises and to provide reports on the results of the safety and security testing.
- Developed guidance and tools for managing AI risk.
- Established the AI Safety and Security Board to advise the Secretary of Homeland Security on the safe and secure use of AI in critical infrastructure.
- Launched the National AI Research Resource (NAIRR) pilot to provide research and education community access to compute and other AI resources.
- Established two NSF-led AI Research Institutes to develop AI tools to advance progress across economic sectors, science, and engineering.

In absence of a federal mandate, some states have started to implement their own rules. For example, on September 28, 2024, Governor Gavin Newsom of California signed Assembly Bill No. 2013 into law, requiring AI developers to disclose the training data used to train the generative AI model.[8]

In the prior chapters of the book, we have also explored the frameworks and good practices that some of the tech companies have put in place. While good progress has been made, there is no guarantee that any of the companies will continue to follow through with the voluntary commitments. Can we truly count on self-regulation—which amounts to nothing more than goodwill—for a technology as powerful and impactful as AI, especially given the intense competitive landscape, the state of capital markets, and the pressure from potential change in direction from the White House given the new administration in 2025? More on the latter in Chapter 10.

It is important to remember that while the US has one of the largest and most active AI ecosystems in the world, many jurisdictions are evolving rapidly. To ensure that the technology can provide benefits for everyone, it is critical that we collaborate across borders. For the rest of the chapter, we will explore the AI governance framework in different countries.

Looking Abroad

While calls for tighter rules and regulations on AI continue to grow, it is easier said than done. Even though AI has been around for a while, as we have talked about throughout this book, the interest around the technology has skyrocketed since the release of ChatGPT in late 2022, and along with it, an AI arms race. As of August 2024, the tool has amassed more than 200 million weekly active users.[9] Incumbent technology firms including Microsoft, Alphabet, Apple, and Meta, as well as startups such as the likes of OpenAI (backed by Microsoft), Anthropic, and Mistral have invested heavily in the space. The speed of change has vastly outpaced the traditional regulatory structures and existing expertise—rendering them ill-equipped to address the potential challenges presented by the technology landscape today.

The question at present becomes, how can we even begin to introduce a framework that can address not only the issues that we see today—including misinformation, deepfakes, copyright, and privacy—but also what we do not know and cannot yet predict? And how can we best model it in a way that encourages collaboration between countries? After all, it is simply unrealistic to have a single nation be the voice and set the standard for a technology with such vast impact transcending physical borders.

Could we, perhaps, create a unilateral baseline agreement that begins with something akin to the Three Laws of Robotics described in Chapter 1 of this book, where robots cannot harm humans nor allow humans to be harmed?

AI Treaty

In September 2024, the first global treaty on AI—The Council of Europe Framework Convention on Artificial Intelligence and Human Rights, Democracy, and the Rule of Law—was open for signature.[10] The work started in 2019 and the Framework Convention was drafted by the 46 member states of the Council of Europe, with participation of all observer states (including Canada, Japan, Mexico, the Holy See, and the US), as well as the EU, and other non-member states.[11] It was signed by Andorra, Georgia, Iceland, Norway, the Republic of Moldova, San Marino, the UK, as well as Israel, the US, and the EU. While this is a legally binding agreement to the countries who sign it, and it covers the use of AI by public authorities and private actors, much is still unknown at this point, including consequences for violation. Nevertheless, this is a good step forward for the global innovation community.

NATO's AI Strategy

Speaking of global impact, the North Atlantic Treaty Organization (NATO) has set out a strategic vision that merits attention. There are four aims and six outcomes included in the strategy, grounded by six principles of responsible use for AI in defense: Lawfulness, Responsibility and Accountability, Explainability and Traceability, Reliability, Governability and Bias Mitigation.[12] While this is a rapidly evolving space, the goal of the strategy document is to provide a foundation for NATO and allies to lead by example, and to encourage responsible AI development and use, for defense and security purposes.

This strategy builds on the initial one published in 2021, considering the rapid development in AI, including generative AI. It specifically calls out a few issues that merit attention, including diminishing availability of quality data that can be used to train AI models, intensive resource demands, as well as adversarial interference including disinformation, information operations, and gender-based violence.

EU Artificial Intelligence Act

The EU Artificial Intelligence Act is the first and most comprehensive AI regulation in the world.[13] It categorizes AI applications into four risk categories.

- Applications that present unacceptable risk and threaten people's rights, such as manipulative AI, social scoring applications, and facial recognition databases compiled by untargeted scraping of facial images from CCTV, are prohibited.
- Applications that are considered high-risk, such as systems that profile individuals using automated processing of personal data to assess different aspects of an individual's life, including economic situation and work performance, are subject to a set of legal requirements, including risk management, data governance, and human oversight. This is the category of AI systems that are the most regulated, since they have the potential to cause harm if they are misused or do not perform as designed.
- There is a smaller group of AI systems that are considered limited risk and are subjected to less regulations and light transparency obligations; humans must be informed that they are interacting with AI (chatbots and deepfakes).
- The rest of the applications, such as spam filters and AI-enabled video games, are considered minimal risk and can be deployed without additional restrictions.

It is worth noting that the requirements associated with the EU AI Act will be applied gradually over time, starting in February 2025 and through 2030, with different transition periods based on different types of systems outlined in the AI Act.[14] It is applicable to not only entities inside the EU but those that outside of the EU as well, if the AI system is used in the EU or impacts those living in the EU. So even if only the output generated by the AI system is used in the EU, both entities that develop and deploy the AI system, including those who reside in the US, may be subjected to the EU AI Act. Non-compliance can result in substantial fines.[15]

In the meantime, a Swiss startup LatticeFlow AI and their partners ETH Zurich and INSAIT, has developed a LLM Checker to test existing models that are on the market for compliance with the AI Act.[16] This will be a valuable tool as the rules continue to be rolled out.

China

Interim Measures for the Management of Generated Artificial Intelligence Services came into effect in August 2023 in China after being reviewed and approved by the 12th Chamber Meeting of the National Internet Information Office on May 23, 2023.[17] Similar to the EU AI Act, the AI Measures in

China are applicable to companies when they provide generative AI services to people within mainland China, regardless of where they are incorporated. Providers are required to apply to the Cyberspace Administration of China (CAC) for security assessment before they can provide generative AI services to the public.[18]

Since the AI Measures are not targeted toward a specific industry, separate regulations and guidance are put in place for different sectors, including financial services. For example, in November 2023, People's Bank of China issued guidelines for the disclosure of AI algorithm for financial applications.

Hong Kong

Unlike mainland China, there are no specific laws or mandatory requirements that govern the development or the use of AI in Hong Kong. In 2019, the Hong Kong Monetary Authority (HKMA) has created a set of guiding principles around consumer protection with respect to the use of big data analytics and AI, focusing on governance and accountability, fairness, transparency and disclosure, and data privacy and protection. In response to the rapid market development and interest in generative AI, the regulator has issued additional guidance in August 2024 to ensure appropriate safeguards for consumer protection are in place when generative AI is adopted for customer-facing applications.[19]

In June 2024, the Office of the Privacy Commissioner for Personal Data (PCPD) issued a model framework called "Artificial Intelligence: Model Personal Data Protection Framework", that aims to provide guidance for organizations that procure, implement, and use AI systems that involve personal data.[20] It builds on the Guidance on the Ethical Development and Use of Artificial Intelligence published in August 2021, which focuses on three core data stewardship values: being respectful, beneficial, and fair; and seven ethical principles for AI: accountability, human oversight, transparency and interpretability, data privacy, beneficial AI, fairness, as well as reliability, robustness, and security.

Unlike the EU AI Act, however, the Model Framework is not a law; rather it seeks to guide organizations on compliance with existing data protection principles and ensuring good data governance practices. From a high-level perspective, the risk-based framework encourages organizations to establish AI strategy and governance (including training), conduct a comprehensive risk assessment and ensure human oversight, ensure data security, and foster regular communications with stakeholders to promote transparency and build trust.[21]

Under the current guidance with respect to responsible use of AI in financial services, financial institutions are encouraged to adopt a risk-based approach in the procurement, use, and management of AI, and ensure human oversight to mitigate potential risks.[22]

Australia

The Australian Government has issued a set of voluntary AI safety standards in September 2024 to help organizations safely and responsibly develop and deploy AI. Mapped alongside these voluntary standards are a set of eight AI Ethics Principles,[23] which include:

- Human, societal, and environmental wellbeing
- Human-centered values
- Fairness
- Privacy protection and security
- Reliability and safety
- Transparency and explainability
- Contestability
- Accountability

These standards were developed by the government in collaboration with the industry, as part of a larger agenda that includes the development of mandatory guardrails for high-risk applications.[24] It should be noted that unlike the EU AI Act, the Australian AI safety standards are not new legal obligations, and they are voluntary—with the understanding that there are already existing laws that are applicable to different AI use cases, e.g. data privacy and anti-discrimination laws.

At the time of writing this chapter, there is an ongoing effort to seek public responses on a set of proposed mandatory guardrails for AI in high-risk settings.

A Fragmented World

Ensuring AI safety requires collaboration from all stakeholders—and progress is possible if we are willing to cast aside our own short-term self-interests—instead of viewing AI as an arms race. The landmark UK AI Safety Summit, held in 2023, was the first high-profile global effort around AI safety, and brought about the Bletchley Declaration, a joint commitment by leaders from 28 countries and the EU to develop AI in a safe and responsible manner.[25] The AI Seoul Summit, held in May 2024, expanded the prior scope to include innovation and inclusivity, as the number of AI safety institutes grows.

Given the current political climate and sentiment, it would be naïve, of course, to ignore the tensions amongst countries, especially between the US and China, and potential spillover effect that threatens to fragment the world and forces countries to take sides. We will likely see a bigger rift between the EU and the US over AI regulations, given the divergent approaches that the two jurisdictions have embarked on, with the stricter approach by the EU on one end, and a hodgepodge approach by the US on the other. The potential impact on US companies operating in EU can be substantial though.

As we continue to navigate the path of innovation, I do hope that we can find ways to overcome our differences and keep the original cooperative spirit alive, to ensure human-centric, trustworthy, inclusive, and responsible AI development to benefit all. From talent to investment, application, and governance, there is more work to be done to move commitment to actions and positive impact. And there is such an immense amount of benefits that we can harness from the technology—if we are willing to share knowledge and work together.

Time is of essence.

Conversation with Aditi Subbarao—Global Financial Services Lead at Instabase

Incorporating AI into legacy processes and infrastructure is no easy task. To start, you need to ask yourself these three questions: Why, where, and Who & How.

First, let's start with: Why. Why are we trying to do it and what is our true objective? There is a lot of AI experimentation being done in the financial services space to just keep up with the Joneses, out of FOMO, because your customers or shareholders expect you to, or just so you can create some marketing buzz around how innovative you are. But true value and benefits from AI can only be achieved when there is a robust underlying objective, where AI is just an enabling tool to meet that objective; it is an enabler and a means to an end, but not the end itself. Figuring this out sets the foundation of your entire AI experience, and this can quite possibly be the single biggest determinant of the level of success you will achieve in the journey.

Next, you will need to figure out 'where'. Think of where AI can help you make a difference. Again, that difference needs to be aligned to the 'why'. If your objective is to improve customer experience, you might want to think twice about redeploying everyone in your customer service team and replacing them with an AI chatbot. Evaluate what your organization is capable of and choose the best path forward. It can be using AI to automate and improve an existing process, or it can be using AI to rethink and completely redesign the process.

Finally, for any tech adoption to succeed, especially in the AI space, it is critical to know who is responsible for the outcomes. AI projects are cross-functional like most other large-scale transformation projects; but often, it involves a lot more rethinking of baselines. Organization structures are being changed to create new AI teams and Chief Data and Analytics Officer (CDAO) roles. It is critical to know where the buck stops, and make sure KPIs and incentives are aligned accordingly. And don't forget your teams and your partners; to be successful, this needs to be a joint effort.

An AI implementation journey can be long and volatile. The technology is changing fast, your customer expectations are changing fast as well. The competitive environments are evolving quickly, so your entire business model is going to change much more quickly than before. Whatever you plan for now, do it with that long-term lens, or at least, keep putting your head up occasionally to look ahead rather than get locked up in only the immediate projects at hand.

We will also see more regulations in data, following GDPR and CCPA. The irony is, the rate of data creation is also increasing exponentially; so, every time you ask AI to create a random poem or picture for you, you are creating so much more data that is technically yours to protect. At the same time, individuals are also becoming more aware of their data and its value. Now it becomes a question of whose responsibility is it to safeguard the data, while still leveraging it responsibly, and how does that sit between the consumers and organizations? What is encouraging though is that we are seeing increasing effort and investment go into access controls, encryption, cybersecurity, and privacy.

Looking ahead, I am excited about the immense gains in returns, risk management, and customer outcomes that can be achieved by being able to search and access all the data within the organization. We will see more personalization of products and services, customized advice, better portfolio and balance sheet risk management, better compliance, and better investments. I am also enthusiastic about the future of agentic AI: Truly distributed and federated execution of actions autonomously by AI Agents. Imagine the productivity gains we have enjoyed so far from implementing AI in banking; now increase that by an order of magnitude. We have been talking about client journeys and data journeys; this is truly reimagining banking as a business model altogether. Watch this space!

Notes

1. J Stempel, NY Times sues OpenAI, Microsoft for infringing copyrighted works, Reuters, 27 December 2023. https://www.reuters.com/legal/transactional/ny-times-sues-openai-microsoft-infringing-copyrighted-work-2023-12-27/
2. D Chmielewski and K Paul, Murdoch's Dow Jones, New York Post sue Perplexity AI for 'illegal' copying of content, Reuters, 21 October 2024. https://www.reuters.com/legal/murdoch-firms-dow-jones-new-york-post-sue-perplexity-ai-2024-10-21/
3. Blackburn, Cantwell, Heinrich Introduce Legislation to Combat AI Deepfakes & Put Journalists, Artists & Songwriters Back in Control of Their Content, Marsha Blackburn, U.S. Senator for Tennessee, 12 July 2024. https://www.blackburn.senate.gov/2024/7/issues/technology/blackburn-cantwell-heinrich-introduce-legislation-to-combat-ai-deepfakes-put-journalists-artists-songwriters-back-in-control-of-their-content
4. I Fried, Lego says its use of AI-generated images was a mistake, Axios, 15 March 2024. https://www.axios.com/2024/03/15/lego-ai-ninjago-images
5. S Parvini, Video game performers will go on strike over artificial intelligence concerns, AP, 26 July 2024. https://apnews.com/article/sagaftra-video-game-performers-ai-strike-4f4c7d846040c24553dbc2604e5b6034
6. FACT SHEET: Biden-Harris Administration Secures Voluntary Commitments from Eight Additional Artificial Intelligence Companies to Manage the Risks Posed by AI, The White house, 12 September

2023. https://www.whitehouse.gov/briefing-room/statements-releases/ 2023/09/12/fact-sheet-biden-harris-administration-secures-voluntary-commitments-from-eight-additional-artificial-intelligence-companies-to-manage-the-risks-posed-by-ai/

7. Fact Sheet: Key AI Accomplishments in the Year Since the Biden-Harris Administration's Landmark Executive Order, The White House, 30 October 2024. https://www.whitehouse.gov/briefing-room/statements-releases/2024/10/30/fact-sheet-key-ai-accomplishme nts-in-the-year-since-the-biden-harris-administrations-landmark-exe cutive-order/

8. AB-2013 Generative artificial intelligence: training data trans-parency.(2023–2024), California Legislative Information, 30 September 2024. https://leginfo.legislature.ca.gov/faces/billNavCl ient.xhtml?bill_id=202320240AB2013

9. I Fried, OpenAI says ChatGPT usage has doubled since last year, Axios, 29 August 2024. https://www.axios.com/2024/08/29/openai-chatgpt-200-million-weekly-active-users

10. Council of Europe, 5 September 2024. https://www.coe.int/en/web/ portal/-/council-of-europe-opens-first-ever-global-treaty-on-ai-for-sig nature

11. The Framework Convention on Artificial Intelligence, Council of Europe, n.d. https://www.coe.int/en/web/artificial-intelligence/the-fra mework-convention-on-artificial-intelligence

12. Summary of NATO's revised Artificial Intelligence (AI) strategy, North Atlantic Treaty Organization, 10 July 2024. https://www.nato.int/cps/ en/natohq/official_texts_227237.htm

13. The EU Artificial Intelligence Act, n.d. https://artificialintelligenceac t.eu/

14. Implementation Timeline, EU Artificial Intelligence Act, n.d. https:// artificialintelligenceact.eu/implementation-timeline/

15. EU Artificial Intelligence Act, n.d. https://artificialintelligenceact.eu/ article/99/

16. M Coulter, EU AI Act checker reveals Big Tech's compliance pitfalls, Reuters, 16 October 2024. https://www.reuters.com/tec hnology/artificial-intelligence/eu-ai-act-checker-reveals-big-techs-com pliance-pitfalls-2024–10-16/?ref = platformer.news.

17. Interim Measures for the Management of Generated Artificial Intelli-gence Services, CAC, 13 July 2023. https://www.cac.gov.cn/2023-07/ 13/c_1690898327029107.htm

18. China: Generative AI Measures Finalized, Library of Congress, 18 July 2023. https://www.loc.gov/item/global-legal-monitor/2023-07-18/china-generative-ai-measures-finalized/

19. Consumer Protection in respect of Use of Generative Artificial Intelligence, Hong Kong Monetary Authority, 19 August 2024. https://www.hkma.gov.hk/media/eng/doc/key-information/guidelines-and-circular/2024/20240819e1.pdf

20. Artificial Intelligence: Model Personal Data Protection Framework, Office of the Privacy Commissioner for Personal Data, Hong Kong, 11 June 2024. https://www.pcpd.org.hk/english/resources_centre/publications/files/ai_protection_framework.pdf

21. Privacy Commissioner's Office Publishes "Artificial Intelligence: Model Personal Data Protection Framework", Office of the Privacy Commissioner for Personal Data, Hong Kong, 11 June 2024. https://www.pcpd.org.hk/english/news_events/media_statements/press_20240611.html

22. Government issues Policy Statement on Responsible Application of Artificial Intelligence in Financial Market, The Government of the Hong Kong Special Administrative Region, 28 October 2024. https://www.info.gov.hk/gia/general/202410/28/P2024102800154.htm

23. Australia's AI Ethics Principles, Australian Government Department of Industry, Science and Resources, n.d. https://www.industry.gov.au/publications/australias-artificial-intelligence-ethics-principles/australias-ai-ethics-principles

24. Voluntary AI Safety Standard, Australian Government Department of Industry, Science and Resources, 5 September 2024. https://www.industry.gov.au/publications/voluntary-ai-safety-standard.

25. The Bletchley Declaration by Countries Attending the AI Safety Summit, GOV.UK, 1 November 2023. https://www.gov.uk/government/publications/ai-safety-summit-2023-the-bletchley-declaration/the-bletchley-declaration-by-countries-attending-the-ai-safety-summit-1-2-november-2023.

10

Trustworthy and Human-Centered AI

How we treat those who are the most vulnerable amongst us will be the ultimate test of our humanity.

In this final chapter, we will showcase examples of organizations that innovate at the intersection of AI and humanity, and how technology can help us reimagine a new future, in banking and beyond.

We will close with a call to action for everyone—from policymakers and innovators to business leaders and citizens of the world. AI is for all—and each of us has a role to play (Fig. 10.1).

© The Author(s), under exclusive license to Springer Nature
Switzerland AG 2025
T. Lau, *Banking on (Artificial) Intelligence*, https://doi.org/10.1007/978-3-031-81647-5_10

TRUSTWORTHY AND HUMAN-CENTERED AI

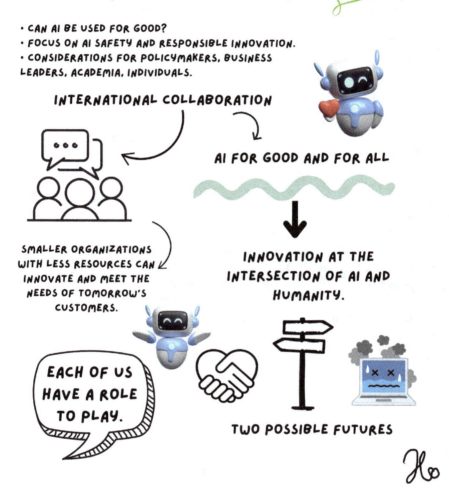

- CAN AI BE USED FOR GOOD?
- FOCUS ON AI SAFETY AND RESPONSIBLE INNOVATION.
- CONSIDERATIONS FOR POLICYMAKERS, BUSINESS LEADERS, ACADEMIA, INDIVIDUALS.

INTERNATIONAL COLLABORATION

AI FOR GOOD AND FOR ALL

SMALLER ORGANIZATIONS WITH LESS RESOURCES CAN INNOVATE AND MEET THE NEEDS OF TOMORROW'S CUSTOMERS.

INNOVATION AT THE INTERSECTION OF AI AND HUMANITY.

EACH OF US HAVE A ROLE TO PLAY.

TWO POSSIBLE FUTURES

Fig. 10.1 Trustworthy and human-centered AI

A Transformative Moment

The most interesting aspect about writing a book on such a fast-paced technology is that I get the opportunity to tap the supportive network of experts in our ecosystem, from startups and credit unions to big tech and incumbent banks.

While we all come from varied lived experiences in different corners of the world, we are all here together at this moment, bearing witness to an important turning point of not only our industry, but of our society.

We have seen different cycles of technology innovation in the past decades. The iPhone is still, in my opinion, one of the big tipping points in our recent history, that has greatly altered the way we live and work, and how we consume services. The fintech industry has been one of the biggest benefactors of the shift.

As I wrote in the beginning of the book, I strongly believe that AI can very well be the same iPhone moment for the current generation, with the potential to change every aspect of our lives. No rocks will be left unturned. The question is, how will we adapt and what can we do to make sure that it can benefit more of humankind? What do we choose to do with the power that we have?

International Collaboration

From the watershed moment when ChatGPT was launched, a powerful force has been unleashed, kicking off the arms race between companies and to some extent—between nations—as they try to outcompete each other. We have seen divergence of opinion when it comes to regulations, with the EU and China, taking a firmer stance toward consumer protection, and the US with a hodgepodge and lighter approach that hinges on the White House Executive Order and voluntary commitments.

Despite the fragmented regulatory and innovation landscape, there is a growing recognition of the risks and benefits brought about by technology. Such challenges and opportunities transcend borders and cultures; solving them will require collaboration between the brightest minds through common standards and a global multi-stakeholder approach that includes not only the governments, but also academia, private sector, researchers, and citizens. And I am heartened to see the momentum on national and global levels to commit to the pursuit of safe and responsible AI—after all, data and technology have no borders. We are in it together.

- Global Partnership on Artificial Intelligence (GPAI): The original Global Partnership on Artificial Intelligence (GPAI) was established in 2020. It counted 29 countries as members—with the goal of fostering exchanges between policymakers and AI experts. The new version of GPAI, announced at the New Delhi Summit in July 2024, brings the OECD members and GAPI countries together, including 44 countries total across six continents, with the goal of advancing human-centric, safe, secure, and trustworthy AI.[1] In addition, various countries including the US, UK, Canada, Singapore, and Japan have established AI Safety Institutes, forming an international network focused on advancing AI safety.[2]
- Partnership on AI (PAI): Partnership on AI is a non-profit partnership with a mission of bringing global diverse voices together, across disciplines and demographics, to drive responsible use of AI. It includes members from academic, civil society, industry, and media organizations—such as American Civil Liberties Union (ACLU), DeepMind, Microsoft, Apple, Amazon, IBM, and OpenAI.[3]
- AI Safety Fund (AISF): The AI Safety Fund makes grant for independent researchers with the goal to promote safe and responsible development of frontier models. The initiative is funded by tech companies such as Anthropic, Google, Microsoft, and OpenAI, as well as philanthropic organizations including Patrick J. McGovern Foundation, David and Lucile Packard Foundation, Schmidt Sciences, and Jaan Tallin. The first round of grants—for twelve grantees across four countries—were awarded in summer 2024.[4]
- Advanced Research + Invention Agency (ARIA): ARIA is a UK-based funding agency to invest in potentially transformative scientific and technological breakthroughs. One of their latest projects, with £59 m in funding, is called Safeguarded AI, which aims to build an AI system that can understand and reduce the risks of other AI agents, and develop safety guarantees to minimize harm.

From Transactions to Relationships

Earlier in Chapter 2, we featured the story of Casca, an AI startup that partners with financial institutions to improve the small business lending experience. In my conversation with Lukas Haffer, CEO of Casca, he recounted the story of apoBank, a German cooperative bank founded in 1902 for doctors, pharmacists, and healthcare professionals. The bank provides financial services for medical students, including student loans, current and savings accounts, credit card, and travel insurance. It also taps into the expertise of the member network, matches graduates of the medical schools with existing healthcare professionals, helps them secure loans for their new practices, and provides wealth management services for their members as they progress along their professional journeys. Not only does such an approach help foster direct relationships between the members in the medical community and the credit union, but it can also reduce the risk in underwriting the new loans.

The hyper focus on relationship and long lens on the member's journey provides a glimpse on the future of banking—one that leverages data to drive a customer-centric experience.

Spotlight on Tiffani Montez, Principal Analyst at EMARKETER
No one can evangelize the transition to life-stage based banking better than Tiffani Montez, Principal Analyst at EMARKETER and banking industry veteran.

If we take the transactions in life and plot the touchpoints over time, what will we see when we connect them and where are the opportunities to serve them better? Take mortgage financing as an example. After initial loan approval, the only likely touchpoint that the financial institution will ever have with the homeowner over span of 15 or 30 years is probably when the mortgage payment comes due: once a month. Imagine the changes that transpire in the life of the account holders and their families, not just the major milestones that they celebrate, but in their daily work and life, over such a long period of time.

"These moments represent the missed opportunities for us to get a better understanding of the customer's life," Tiffani suggested, "and a way for us to offer them personalized advice and services—when and where it matters— that can help them realize their long-term goals beyond securing the initial loan and buying the property." Tiffani called this customer-centric banking model life stage-based banking.

Instead of catering for a transaction or a "Gen-Z" experience based on an artificial bracket around the number of birthday candles, imagine expanding the flywheel to different touchpoints in the consumer's life, such as a car purchase and relocation, and extending it through their various life stages.

Building such an experience outside traditional banking services will require us to look at customer experience in a different way, however. We need to be willing to invest in fostering a long-term relationship with the customer beyond the initial financial transaction, which will likely upend our traditional business models. We also need access to a vast amount of data across industries. In this new paradigm, we will need to be able to integrate

> the data in a fashion that can enable us to draw useful insights from it and offer complementary non-financial services that are relevant to the customer's life stage.

I don't have a crystal ball into the future. But if I were to make an educated guess, this will likely require an entity with modern data infrastructure, and one with brand trust and affinity. Will this usher in a new era of banking services for the incumbents or big technology firms? What role will regulations play in enabling this new future? And what will become of the financial institutions with heavy tech debt and limited access to talent and resources?

Instead of re-engineering services based on how we interact with our financial institutions today, which are limited by legacy infrastructure, emerging technologies have provided us an opportunity to re-imagine a new and different relationship: One that is based on trust and our focus on delivering value to our customers and members. How we craft the story—figuratively and literally—will dictate how the next story will be written.

There is No AI Without Data

What does this evolution mean to the legacy platforms and core systems? Will middleware control the future of banking? Granted, we are still in the very beginning of a transition, and we are still quite a few years away before we see substantial change in banking models. But change is happening in different corners of our ecosystem—banks that have strong data infrastructure will be able to leapfrog their competitors and innovate faster to not only meet, but anticipate their customers' demands.

"We are moving toward an applied capabilities era, where embedded finance will expand the financial services industry broadly. Nobody is quite sure where that's going, you can tell who is planning ahead. AI-ready banks will have clear control of their customer and operational data. They will know who, what, when, where, and why any critical data is used and adapt their strategy accordingly." Commented Patrick Rivenbark, banking and payments industry veteran.

Indeed, with the increasingly competitive ecosystem, banks can no longer afford to sit on the sidelines or be held hostage by what their legacy systems can support. Significant opportunities exist for companies who can provide the tools for banks to access and connect the dots and become data ready.

A Brighter Future

There are glimmers of hope in different corners of our ecosystem.

Take the case of Commonwealth Bank in Australia for instance, which has developed an AI model to help identify digital payment transactions that include harassing, threatening, or offensive messages. As our world moves digital, so have the perpetrators who commit financial abuse. After successful deployment in 2021, CommBank has made the code and the model available for free, for banks everywhere in the world, in the hope that more banks will be able to leverage the technology to create safer banking experience for all.[5] This is crucial as financial abuse is costly—both from a monetary perspective as well as from a mental and physical perspective. American Banker reported that the yearly cost from financial abuse stands around $3.7 billion in Australia and $28 billion in the US in 2022.[6]

Another interesting example comes from Ant Group, which has revolutionized QR code payments with Alipay and took the world by storm with its super app two decades ago. Recently, the big tech launched Maxiaocai—its new AI financial manager that can be accessed via the Alipay app and Ant Fortune app. The AI assistant uses Ant Group's LLM capabilities and partners with over 200 financial institutions to deliver customized financial services for their 70 million monthly active users.[7]

Spotlight on Great Lakes Credit Union

Great Lakes Credit Union (GLCU), founded in 1938, is a not-for-profit financial cooperative with over $1.6 billion in assets, serving more than 95,000 members in Chicagoland and surrounding areas. For GLCU, the most challenging part when it comes to partnering with AI startups is regulatory uncertainty. According to Elizabeth Osborne, Chief Operations Officer of GLCU, financial institutions, especially credit unions, are hesitant to deploy new AI-driven models without clear guidance from the regulators. As such, their credit union had to take extra precautionary measures during contract negotiations with their AI provider.

When it comes to vendor selection, one of the key factors that GLCU must consider is whether the AI provider has prior experience integration with their core system. Integration issues remain one of the top technical and operational challenges when it comes to digital transformation efforts. When vetting potential AI partners, Elizabeth also noted that it is essential to treat them as critical (tech) vendors, to ensure transparency and that the proper due diligence process is followed. Alignment on vision is also crucial as the model needs to be maintained and updated.

Establishing and maintaining trust is paramount for our industry, and actions speak louder than words. Consistency, commitment to excellence, and education, are all key to establishing trust in AI. As Olive, the call center virtual AI assistant used by Great Lakes Credit Union, demonstrates, when technology is deployed thoughtfully and responsibly, it can provide great value-add for credit union members and their operations staff. For example:

- Olive consistently fully handles over 60% of total inbound calls during business hours and over 75% of all calls after business hours, compared to a less than 25% handling rate with the previous "telephone banking" solution, which did not include AI technology.
- Olive has increased the number of calls fully serviced by the virtual assistant by over 200% since launch.

Beyond conversational AI chatbots, tremendous potential exists for AI to help solve some of the industry's bigger challenges, including fraud and loan decisioning. The question isn't if financial institutions should embark on the journey; rather, it should be how. And the onus should be on the stakeholders in the ecosystem to ensure that institutions of all sizes, as well as their members, can benefit equally from the technology innovation.

Talking to credit union executives such as Elizabeth Osborne gives me comfort in knowing that there are strong leaders in our communities that understand the importance of customer-centricity in a tech-enabled world driven by data intelligence. Ability to strike the balance between pursuing innovation and maintaining the human touch is increasingly critical, especially as technology is increasingly being exploited by bad actors to cause harm to ordinary citizens. Our sense of shared responsibility and duty to care—the unique traits that make us human—is the best antidote to the tidal waves of threats to come.

An Alternate Future

If we pause for a moment and think back to the vision from the early internet days—where we dreamt about a digital world that would not be restricted by physical borders. That almost felt like a distant past. The more connected we are, the more echo chambers we create, and the more splintered our society has become.

The fragmented legislative landscape is most apparent when it comes to the types of technologies that people in different countries have access to. At the time of writing, Apple's on-device AI system, known as Apple Intelligence, for example, is not available in the EU if the user's Apple Account Country / Region is in the EU; and the tech giant is naming the Digital Markets Act as the culprit. The service is also not available in mainland China as Apple still must clear regulatory hurdles with the local authorities.

Against the backdrop of national policies and relentless pursuit of profits over purpose, what will the future hold? Can AI truly be used to as an equalizer and create positive value for everyone? Or will it be exploited yet as another tool to generate wealth and control for the powerful and the rich?

As I pen this final chapter, the US presidential election has just wrapped up. And we will see a new administration in early 2025. As big companies in the tech and banking industries reposition themselves for the new administration post-election, a different picture is slowly emerging in terms of the future of AI development. While it might still be too early to tell and things can and will continue to evolve, here are a few scenarios where things may play out.

- Talent constraints: While the previous two AI winters were centered around technical issues and costs, for the not-too-distant future, we will likely run into talent constraints—due to competition of talent between big tech, startups, government, and academia, as well as a potential tightening of immigration policies from the new administration. From a business perspective, organizations need to find pathways to upskilll and reskill their current workforce, and the career pathways of the existing workforce also need rethinking. Education needs to be revamped to nurture creative thinking and other skills that will be vital for the AI-led future.

- Resource drain and environment impact: Another constraint we will very soon run into is power. Training and operating AI models require a massive amount of electricity. The US has a third of the world's data centers, but our energy infrastructure is outdated and cannot support the data center needs. At the same time, big tech needs to fulfill their clean energy goals. These two pressures will cause the utility companies to look for different ways to generate electricity, and we have already seen big tech companies including Google, Microsoft and OpenAI looking for alternatives including nuclear. Banks will become both the consumers and the enablers (funders) in this scenario. With the new administration's agenda, however, it is unclear if the pursuit of clean energy alternatives will continue or how, and the potential impact on the environment if we choose a different route to satisfy our energy needs.

- Corporate alliances (and the big becomes bigger): As we have iterated in previous chapters, size and scale matter, not just for banks but also big tech companies. To leverage AI to its fullest potential, the organizations need access to data, resources, and talent. We have seen how GAFA has evolved into Magnificent Seven, and how the top banks have dominated the AI innovation landscape. As anti-trust regulations get relaxed under the new administration, we will likely see more big techs coupling up with big banks as well as more merger and acquisition activities between incumbents and startups. However, this can potentially create higher barriers of entry for small organizations to develop and adopt AI.

- Global disparities: Without corrective action, we will continue to see bigger divide between the wealthy and the poor, and between global north and global south. As countries such as China explore less resource-intensive ways of developing AI, they will turn to open source and small language models (SLMs instead of LLMs), which will likely become a model for the smaller developing nations. We have seen countries in the Middle East investing heavily in frontier technologies, and governments leading initiatives to make sure their languages and cultures will not be left behind. However, how will the nations with less digital footprint and low-resource languages be included in this future AI-led world? Who will stand up for those who don't have a voice at the table? The pathway remains unclear.

- Fragmented regulations: We are already seeing the beginning of the arms race between companies and between countries. The complex regulatory landscape can pose challenges to organizations that work globally. Digital has no physical borders, and a fragmented approach creates immense challenges for trusted and regulated industries such as banking and does little to safeguard the well-being of consumers. With incoming administration likely to become even more hands-off when it comes to regulations, and they have already signaled their intention to dismantle the AI safeguards in the White House Executive Order, the fate of the remaining 120 AI bills in US Congress is unknown. Will we see a reversal of prior efforts around responsible AI development? How will this impact the collaboration amongst nations and the progress that has been made (Fig. 10.2)?

FACTORS INFLUENCING FUTURE OF AI DEVELOPMENT

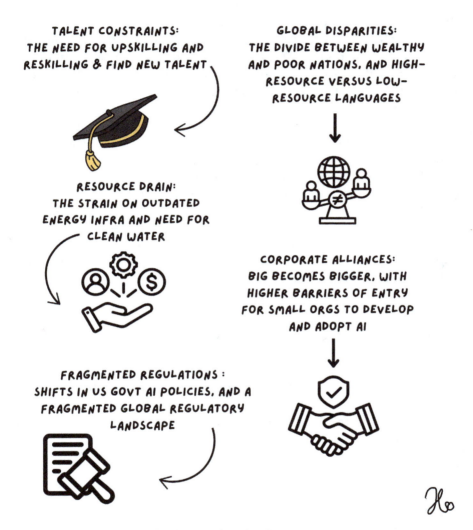

Fig. 10.2 Factors influencing future of AI development

A Journey into the Unknown

While AI can be leveraged to help optimize efficiency at data center operations, it can also be used to maximize production from oil and gas reserves. Just as how AI can be used to close the wealth gap by enabling different pathways to financial security, but at the same time, it can also be exploited to amplify the systemic biases in our system.

Do the benefits offset the harms? I don't know if we would ever find out. But intention drives outcomes. What you choose to invest in, for whom, and why matters. And for so long as technology and the monetary system exists, such duality has been part of the picture as well. The road that we will travel depends on the choices that we make—as individuals, as private entities, and as a country. Will we see a future that celebrates collaboration and intentional actions to promote a fairer and more equitable world? Or will we see a darker version—an alternate future?

There are nuances with each decision we make, and it is not my intention to dictate—as real life is full of asterisks and uncertainties. I hope that this book will help spark dialogue and collaboration not just within our silos but beyond. While the data is 1's and 0's, the Realities of AI is very much human. And it is up to all of us to decide what the future holds.

At the time of publication, the new incoming administration has just rescinded the White House Executive Order on AI. Some of the references to the Biden Administration's work on AI throughout this book may have been archived as a result. It is unclear at this point what the future will hold in terms of federal AI regulations in the US.

Notes

1. Global Partnership on Artificial Intelligence, OECD, n.d. https://www.oecd.org/en/about/programmes/global-partnership-on-artificial-intelligence.html
2. A Variengien and C Martinet, AI Safety Institutes: Can countries meet the challenge? OCED, 29 July 2024. https://oecd.ai/en/wonk/ai-safety-institutes-challenge.
3. Partnership on AI, n.d. https://partnershiponai.org/
4. Update on the AISF Grantmaking and Upcoming Funding Opportunity, AI Safety Fund, November 2024. https://aisfund.org/update-on-the-aisf-grantmaking-and-upcoming-funding-opportunity/
5. In a world first, CBA shares its artificial intelligence model to help reduce technology-facilitated abuse, CommBank, 8 November 2024. https://www.commbank.com.au/articles/newsroom/2023/11/next-chapter-open-artificial-intelligence-model.html

6. J Adams, How one bank uses generative AI to fight domestic abuse, American Banker, 5 December 2023. https://www.americanbanker. com/payments/news/how-one-bank-uses-generative-ai-to-fight-dom estic-abuse
7. Ant Group Unveils AI Financial Manager at Shanghai's INCLUSION Conference, Yahoo! Finance, 6 September 2024. https://finance.yahoo. com/news/ant-group-unveils-ai-financial-052100385.html

Afterword

Brian Lee is the President/CEO at Landings Credit Union

Landings Credit Union has been in business for over 70 years. During that time, there have been all kinds of technological advances that make banking easier and more accessible. I was recently through some old annual reports and our 25th anniversary report in 1978 touted our new "on-line data processing system" that "increased our capabilities to implement member programs". However, the CEO at the time also noted, "Like all automatic systems, it is not foolproof. It does occasionally get contrary and is slower than we would like it to be."

Since the time that was written in 1978, I'm sure I could write volumes about the times new technology became "contrary". For our 50th year in 2003, our credit union launched our new online banking and bill pay service. It had a bit of a curve for implementation and acceptance, but quickly became a useful feature. Improvements over the years in core processing systems, ATMs, online and mobile banking, and payment processing have given our members more tools than ever to manage their finances. At the same time, the credit union has used new systems to improve the processes of opening new accounts, underwriting loans, and processing data.

While technological improvements have certainly created efficiencies and increased our reach, the most important focus remains on the individual, the human on the other side of the digital interaction. So, the question is: how do we deliver a unique and impactful member experience when we no longer have personal interaction with the majority of our members?

I have always thought that an efficient and simple experience for our members is one indicator of excellent member service. On the other hand,

T. Lau, *Banking on (Artificial) Intelligence*, https://doi.org/10.1007/978-3-031-81647-5

there are still times when in-person experiences are necessary and preferable. For example, if I have purchased several cars or homes over my lifetime, I may be comfortable with reviewing and signing documents digitally without much consultation. But there are situations with first-time buyers, older members, or others when they would prefer to meet with a representative.

Once again, the challenge remains of finding solutions that serves all members. When making important decisions in an ever-evolving financial services landscape, we need to ask ourselves, "Who are we leaving behind?"

Artificial Intelligence tools have the potential of significantly expanding how we impact our members' lives. New AI tools for call centers and chatbots understand more languages than we can hire on staff. This creates an environment where members are more comfortable conducting sensitive financial transactions and could make way for decreasing the number of unbanked and underbanked members of our communities. AI underwriting considers more factors than historical underwriting and has the potential for financial institutions to expand lending to more people. AI is also being used to analyze data and find opportunities for us to reach out to members to improve their financial condition.

So why aren't we seeing a more rapid adoption of these tools in financial institutions? For my credit union and many other financial institutions, we are faced with financial constraints, knowledge gaps, and overall distrust of new service providers, which keeps us from fully jumping in.

First of all, many smaller community financial institutions must balance budget constraints as they look for new tools and partnerships. Despite the promises of increased efficiencies or improved revenue, the set up and monthly fees are often cost prohibitive. Taking into account how long it may take to recuperate those costs or how quickly this new technology may become obsolete keeps some of us on the sideline, even when a solution is desired.

Additionally, it takes significant time and resources to properly research, negotiate, implement, and monitor these new services. Whether it's a knowledge gap, talent gap, or just lack of time to stay on top of trends, it's a real concern that financial institutions can't keep up with this fast pace of change.

Finally, I have personally seen the exponential growth of new companies that have entered this arena. For years, it was relatively steady when it came to the vendors that showed up at conferences and built relationships with credit unions. Over the past few years there has been a rapid increase in the number of business development executives contacting me over email, through LinkedIn, or at conferences. It can be very overwhelming to decide when I will accept appointments of "just 10 min" to sort through all the offerings.

I don't mean to sound negative about the innovative companies that are arriving to provide something that we cannot creative ourselves. I mean to draw attention to the hurdles that face in implementing new technology with the ultimate goal of benefitting our members. Flashy new technology in and of itself will not solve all our problems. Any financial institution expecting to add AI to any of their processes without ensuring the policies, procedures, and controls behind the AI are sound is in for a rude awakening. If we rush to implement these new tools without the proper due diligence and follow through, we can expect to see some of these systems get "contrary" just like we did in 1978.

I return to my earlier question of "who are we leaving behind?" and flip that around to ask financial institutions "which of us are getting left behind, and why?". If many financial institutions lack the resources and expertise to keep up with these changes, does that make a future with more and more consolidation? Or, can we find ways to collaborate that will give smaller community institutions opportunities to easily adopt these new tools are remain competitive? Just as we aim to provide a simplified, low-cost, and efficient experience for our members, can vendors find ways to make it easier, cheaper, and more accessible to financial institutions to form these essential partnerships? Let's take advantage of these opportunities for innovation and make sure everyone has an invitation to the table.

Index

GPSR Compliance
The European Union's (EU) General Product Safety Regulation (GPSR) is a set
of rules that requires consumer products to be safe and our obligations to
ensure this.

If you have any concerns about our products, you can contact us on

ProductSafety@springernature.com

In case Publisher is established outside the EU, the EU authorized
representative is:

Springer Nature Customer Service Center GmbH
Europaplatz 3
69115 Heidelberg, Germany